The Best Hiking
in Ontario

Doug Robertson

The Best Hiking
in Ontario

Hurtig Publishers
Edmonton

Hurtig Publishers Ltd.
10560 – 105 Street
Edmonton, Alberta
Canada   T5H 2W7

Canadian Cataloguing in Publication Data

Robertson, Doug, 1949-
   The best hiking in Ontario

Bibliography: p. 137
ISBN 0-88830-256-8

1. Hiking – Ontario – Guide-books.   2. Trails –
Ontario – Guide-books.   3. Ontario – Description and
travel – Guide-books.   I. Title.
GV199.44.C2205 1984   917.13′044   C84-091152-1

Picture Credits:
D. Robertson: 18, 48, 52, 92
L. Gosselin: 63
Ontario Ministry of Natural Resources: 69, 108, 111, 113, 114, 119
Royal Botanical Gardens: 15, 104, 105, 107

Printed and bound in Canada

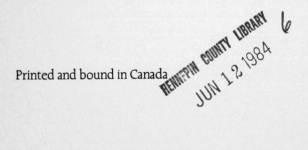

Contents

Acknowledgements

Just as the lives of individuals are shaped and coloured by the personalities and events they are exposed to during their formation and growth, so this book is the product of far more than the author's hand. Indeed, the book could not have come into being without the encouragement, support, and assistance of many friends and family members who frequently offered critical advice, and who gracefully tolerated my idiosyncrasies during the period of manuscript preparation.

I especially want to thank the many staff members of the Ontario Ministry of Natural Resources, Parks Canada, conservation authorities, and the volunteers of the Federation of Ontario Hiking Trail Associations who were so helpful in providing and confirming many important pieces of information.

Of special note are Peter Wanner, whose wizardry with his Osborne I computer made manuscript preparation a breeze, Trevor Stock (editor of the *Bruce Trail Guidebook*), who prepared the maps, and Norman Holt of Oxbow Books (102 Main Street South, Georgetown, L7G 3E4) who generously applied his editing skills by reviewing a draft of the manuscript. I am also grateful for the assistance provided by the staff of Open Air Books and Maps (10 Adelaide Street East, Toronto, M5C 1H5) for their valuable assistance in preparing the useful references listed in "Other Reading" at the end of the book.

Finally, while every effort has been made to ensure that all information in the following pages is correct, I accept full responsibility for any errors or omissions that may have crept in as I distilled a veritable mountain of hiking and nature trail information provided by the managing organizations.

The Trail User's Code

- Hike only along marked routes.
- Do not climb fences — use the stiles.
- Carry out all garbage. (If you can carry it in you can carry it out.)
- Light cooking fires at official campsites only — drench fires after use. (Better still, carry a lightweight hiker's stove.)
- Leave flowers and plants for others to enjoy.
- Never strip bark from trees.
- Keep dogs on the leash, on or near farm land.
- Walk around the edges of fields — not across them.
- Protect and do not disturb wildlife.
- Leave only your thanks and take nothing but photographs.

Introduction

For many outdoor enthusiasts, hiking trails provide a personal challenge; a test of skill and endurance against the elements or perhaps even against fellow hikers. For others, the value of the hiking experience can be measured in the number of kilometres covered or trails completed. Still others find a pleasant, if temporary, escape from the pressure of everyday life on the trails.

All these things are important, but for me trails — whatever their form, length, or destination — offer something more: they allow me access to many of the elements of nature that I enjoy — birds, animals, trees, flowers; indeed to all the sights, sounds, and scents of the living, breathing earth. Hiking trails offer a way to establish and reinforce a certain unity of humanity and nature, a unity that has been badly fractured by the dictates of life in the modern industrialized world.

This book is offered as a key — one of many available — to that natural world. In the following pages, the novice wanting an introduction to Ontario's natural beauty and the experienced hiker seeking expanded horizons will both find the kind of "first-step" information so necessary to a properly planned hiking trip. This book, then, is a directory; a guide to a selection of the best hiking trails in the province.

Rather than provide details on the route and use of each trail or "how-to" advice on hiking technique, equipment, and food (there are excellent books on these subjects listed in the bibliography), I have attempted to fill a gap in the hiker's library by presenting basic information on where trails are and sources from which detailed and current information may be obtained.

To avoid having the book go out of date too quickly I have refrained from quoting specific map prices, membership fees, public transportation fares, park entry and camping fees, hours and dates of operation, etc. Such figures seem to escalate all too frequently these days. While this may mean a little extra work for the hiker, trail managers will no doubt appreciate it. As a manager of the Bruce Trail I have personal experience of the administrative headaches caused by guidebook orders and membership applications based on information as much as ten years out of date.

To the hiker (or hiker-to-be), tourist, naturalist, educator, fitness enthusiast, or just plain rambler: may this book serve you well as a useful hike-planning tool for many years to come.

Ontario's natural beauty and hiking trails await; they are yours to discover.

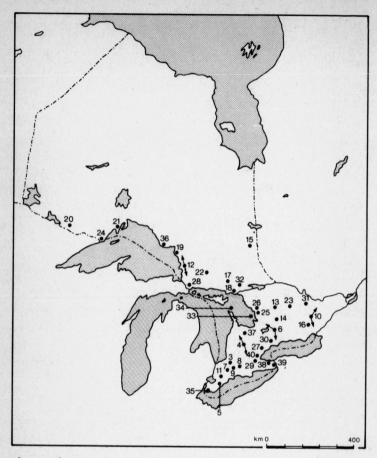

The numbers on the above location map (1)
correspond to numbers assigned to the trail maps
in this book.

Hiking in Ontario

A Thumbnail Geography

Ontario is a vast province stretching over sixteen hundred
kilometres from east to west and over seventeen hundred
kilometres from north to south. As might be expected, the
province's more than one million square kilometres of area
permit a considerable variety of forest cover, geology,
topography, soils, climate, and wildlife, as well as human
settlement patterns.

In the north the muskeg and stunted coniferous forests of
the flat Hudson Bay lowlands — corresponding roughly with
the zone of discontinuous permafrost — are best visited via
the many rivers which meander north from the height of land
separating the Great Lakes and Hudson Bay watersheds. This is
canoe and bush plane country; not for hikers.

Further south, sweeping like a giant horseshoe out of the
Northwest Territories through the upper Great Lakes region
and on into northern Quebec, lie the roots of ancient
Pre-Cambrian mountain ranges known collectively as the
Canadian Shield. These three-and-a-half-billion-year-old rocks,
worn smooth by aeons of wind and rain and several
continental glaciers, hold much of the mineral, forest, and
hydro-electric wealth of the province. But large tracts of
wilderness remain relatively untouched, protected by slowly
growing provincial and national park systems. Parts of this
wilderness, home to black bear, moose, deer, timber wolf,
many smaller mammals, and over a hundred of the 272 species
of birds which nest in Ontario, offer some of the best back-
country hiking anywhere. Good trails such as the Voyageur

Trail, those in Quetico, Lake Superior, Sibley, Killarney, and Algonquin provincial parks, and in Pukaskwa National Park, invite the adventurous and more experienced hiker to try extended backpacking trips among thousands of lakes, rivers, and streams and through some truly breathtaking scenery.

In contrast, the Great Lakes–St. Lawrence lowlands to the south of the rugged Shield offer hundreds of shorter trails better suited to the novice or to the experienced hiker in need of shaping up for greater challenges. But don't be fooled; although this part of the province might be described as a gently rolling, rather pastoral landscape of farms, villages, towns, and small cities, most of southern Ontario's trails have some very wild and rugged sections. And although much of the original forest cover was removed during the 1800s, reforestation of marginal farmland, river valleys, and other areas is gradually expanding the amount of land suitable for hiking, nature study, and other forms of outdoor recreation. Southern Ontario's large urban population has benefitted hikers, in that the area has the most trails and the greatest total length of trails in the province, providing a variety of hiking opportunities in very scenic natural sourroundings. Perhaps variation in the degree of challenge that awaits the hiker is one of the greatest assets of Ontario's hiking trails.

Ontario's trails provide a unique and tranquil access to many facets of the province's cultural and natural mosaic. There is a type of trail for everyone.

Weather & Climate

Ontario is not a mountainous province so hikers need not be concerned about weather extremes arising from elevation differences. Local conditions such as ground fog, heavy dew, or cold-air drainage may be encountered, but such topography-related weather presents little, if any, direct threat to hiker safety.

The province's north-south distances, however, present some significant climatic variations for which the hiker should be prepared. In late winter, for instance, when the northern end of the Voyageur Trail may be locked in deep snow and -30°C temperatures, early spring wildflowers may be blooming in sheltered spots along the southern stretches of the Bruce Trail or along the trails of Point Pelee National Park. In July or

On most trails in Ontario, the joys of hiking can be found in every season.

August, when the southern trails may be wilting under a humid 35°C air mass from the Gulf of Mexico, hikers in Algonquin, Killarney, or Lake Superior provincial parks may shiver at night without a warm sweater and a campfire.

Daily weather fluctuations can be common as well. Ontario's weather is often characterised by two- to five-day cycles of different weather conditions. As a result of *frontogenesis* (the collision of air masses of different temperatures and humidity), the weather at the beginning of an outing might not bear the least similarity to the weather at the end of the trip, a few short days later. This is especially true along the shores of Georgian Bay, Lake Huron, and Lake Superior, where the added factor of a large, relatively cold water body can complicate summer weather mechanisms and produce sudden wind and rain squalls, rapid temperature drops, and major shifts in wind direction.

These are ideal ingredients for hypothermia, the principal danger to hikers during much of the year. (See the section on "Health and Safety Tips.") Hikers should therefore seek out and heed sources of local weather information. Environment Canada, for example, broadcasts continuous weather information via its weather radio service (e.g., Toronto, 162.475 MHz), and local radio and television stations issue detailed and frequent forecasts geared to marine and aviation interests. These can be very useful in planning a day's clothing and equipment requirements.

Rules & Regulations

At the beginning of the book you read the Trail User's Code, a list of the do's and don'ts of hiking. If every hiker who set foot on a trail adhered to the Code, this section could end here. Unfortunately, in spite of considerable efforts by park and trail managers to educate trail users, it can't.

Any outdoor sport which sees growing numbers of people using the wilderness and other natural areas, inevitably calls for rules to be imposed to protect the environment and to reduce conflict with other recreationists and occupiers of the lands being used. This has been especially true in Ontario. Heavy demands on certain provincial parks and recreation facilities have brought about the imposition of can and bottle restrictions, controls on alcohol, pre-registration for some back-country travel and, in 1980, the passing of two new provincial laws: the *Trespass to Property Act* and the *Occupier's Liability Act*.

More will be said about the specific park and trail rules in the detailed trail descriptions to follow, but hikers — especially when using the volunteer trail system where many of the trails cross private land thanks to a handshake agreement between the landowners and the hiking club — must be aware of their legal duties and responsibilities. The survival of many such trails depends on it.

In most circumstances, adherence to the Trail User's Code will satisfy the letter of the law as far as the well-behaved hiker is concerned. Just to be sure, though, both laws are reprinted verbatim in Appendix 1. Hikers should know where they stand and what is expected of them.

In general the *Occupier's Liability Act* is intended to clarify the duties of care owed by landowners to people they have invited onto their property; for instance, hikers using a marked trail in a responsible manner by virtue of an agreement with a trail-managing club. A landowner must do what is reasonable to see that hikers are not injured by the condition of the property or by activities going on there. Hikers, on the other hand, are expected to willingly assume all risks of injury and are deemed to be responsible for their own safety.

The *Trespass to Property Act* is intended to give a landowner greater control over the type of recreational activity on his or her land, and provides for a fine of up to $1,000 upon

Hikers should abide by the Trail User's Code, using stiles to climb fences, for example, as these children are doing.

conviction. A landowner may thus choose to permit only hikers to use the property, or to permit all uses other than hiking, or to permit any other combination of uses depending on his or her wishes. A system of universal signs and markings is recommended for the enforcement of the act.

For the hiker using trails in Ontario, the rule of thumb should be to stay on the clearly marked route, camp only where signs and guidebook instructions indicate camping is permitted, and accept all responsibility for presence on and use of the trail. In other words, the hiker must abide by the Trail User's Code!

Above all, the hiker should afford all possible respect for the land and its owners or managers, and for fellow hikers, whether required to do so by rules or law or not.

Transportation

Most of Ontario's major trails can be reached via public transportation assisted, perhaps, with a little leg work.

In the Toronto region regular bus and train routes cross the Bruce, Guelph, and Ganaraska trails at several points and pass close to several conservation areas. The GO (Government of Ontario) train system, for instance, running from Toronto to Hamilton, to Milton, and to Georgetown, provides cheap access to the Bruce Trail, although the trains operate on commuter-oriented schedules. The GO bus system is even more widespread. The province-wide commercial bus lines (Gray Coach, Greyhound, Voyageur, Charterways, Ontario Northland, etc.) make virtually any trail accessible from Toronto or from the major entry points to Ontario: Buffalo, Detroit, Montreal, Sault Ste. Marie, or from Winnipeg or points west. Many carriers on rural runs will even stop to let off or pick up passengers on demand. Canadian National and Canadian Pacific railways operate a number of passenger-train services connecting the major urban centres in Ontario from where trail access may be made.

For hikers arriving by air, Lester B. Pearson International Airport is on a GO bus run that connects, at its eastern end, with the Toronto Transit Commission's bus and subway systems, and at its western end with Georgetown, near the Bruce Trail. Taxis and car rentals are also available, although the latter should be prearranged. Air Canada, Norontair, and other regional air carriers provide service to all major and many minor centres around the province, allowing hikers to connect with the local public and private bus services.

Hikers with their own vehicles will find that Ontario's highways, county and local roads, open forest access, and park roads allow for literally hundreds of trail access points throughout the province.

Maps

Whatever the mode of transportation, hikers seeking access to Ontario's trail systems should obtain and study two basic maps: a relatively detailed map of Ontario (the Ontario government road map will do) and a detailed map of the trail to be used (e.g., the trail guidebook, provincial park or conservation area map). In addition, the following are further sources of maps and information:

1. Guidebooks and map sets published by volunteer trail management organizations. See the addresses in the individual trail descriptions in Section II.
2. Federal government National Topographic Series maps: 1:50,000 scale for the entire province, 1:25,000 for parts of southern Ontario only. Several larger scales are also available. Get free indexes before ordering maps from:

> Canada Map Office
> Department of Energy, Mines and Resources
> Ottawa, Ontario   K1A 0E9

> Public Service Centre
> Ministry of Natural Resources
> 1st Floor, Whitney Block
> 99 Wellesley Street West
> Toronto, Ontario   M7A 1W3

> Designated retail map outlets in Ontario (usually book stores, sporting goods stores).

3. Provincial and county road maps can be ordered from:

> Ministry of Transportation and Communications
> Record Services Office, East Building
> Downsview, Ontario   M3M 1J8

4. Individual provincial parks and conservation area maps are available from:

> Ministry of Natural Resources
> Parks and Recreation Areas Branch
> 3rd Floor, Whitney Block
> 99 Wellesley Street West
> Toronto, Ontario   M7A 1W3

> District Ministry of Natural Resources offices
> (see list in Appendix 2)

> Local conservation authority offices
> (see list in Appendix 2)

5. National parks maps

> See individual trail descriptions.

Accommodations

While most hikers will want to use the many campsites and shelters along and near Ontario's trails, other forms of accommodation are available for trail users who may not wish to "rough it."

Bed & Breakfast

An idea imported from Britain and Europe, where it has been a part of the tourist economy for decades, bed and breakfast accommodation is fast becoming popular among Canadian hikers.

Rooms, usually located in large private homes, and one or

two hearty meals a day are often available for half the going hotel/motel rates.

Several good directories and registries of bed and breakfast establishments have been published. Three of these are: *Ontario Bed and Breakfast Book*, by Patricia Wilson; *Country Bed and Breakfast Places in Canada*, by John Thompson; and *The Canadian Bed and Breakfast Guide*, by Gerda Pantel. All are available in many public libraries and book shops.

An example of an excellent bed and breakfast referral network is *Country Host*, a chain of private establishments located along the Bruce Trail. For further information contact:

Country Host
R. R. #1
Palgrave, Ontario   L0N 1P0
Telephone (519) 941-7633

Hostels

The Great Lakes Hostelling Association manages several year-round hostels in Ontario and is planning to expand the system. Card-carrying members of the Bruce Trail Association and the Canadian Cycling Association may use all but the Ottawa hostel at the same low rates enjoyed by members of the Hostelling Association — a real deal! Contact the following for information:

Great Lakes Hostelling Association
223 Church Street
Toronto, Ontario   M5B 1Z1
Telephone: (416) 368-1848

Or individual hostels

Toronto
223 Church Street
Toronto, Ontario   M5B 1Z1
Telephone (416) 368-1848

Collingwood
Blue Mountain Hostel
R. R. #3
Collingwood, Ontario   L9Y 3Z2
Telephone (705) 445-1497

Goderich
Black's Point Hostel
R. R. #2
Goderich, Ontario   N7A 3X8
Telephone: (519) 524-2318

Niagara Falls
Niagara Falls Hostel
4699 Zimmerman Avenue
Niagara Falls, Ontario   L2E 3M7
Telephone: (416) 357-0770

Orillia
Orillia Hostel
198 Borland Street East
Orillia, Ontario   L3V 2C3
Telephone: (705) 325-0970

Sault Ste. Marie
L'Auberge de Sault Ste. Marie
452 Bay Street
Sault Ste. Marie, Ontario   P6A 1X2
Telephone: (705) 256-7233

Brantford
Brantford Hostel
40 Queen Street
Brantford, Ontario   N3T 3B2
Telephone: (519) 752-6568

Ottawa
Ottawa Hostel
75 Nicholas Street
Ottawa, Ontario   K1N 7B9
Telephone: (613) 235-2595

Thunder Bay
Longhouse Village Hostel
Lakeshore Drive
R. R. #13
Thunder Bay, Ontario   P7B 5E4
Telephone: (807) 983-2042

Hotels, Motels, Cottages & Lodges

There are hundreds of commercial establishments of these types in Ontario. Many on or near hiking trails have come to see hikers as a major market, especially during "off" seasons. Inquire about rates for off seasons (especially during early spring or late fall) or for members of hiking clubs. The Ontario Ministry of Tourism and Recreation publishes a detailed directory entitled *Accommodations*. Contact the following or visit a local Ontario Travel Information Centre for a free copy:

Ontario Travel Information Centre
Ministry of Tourism and Recreation
1st Floor, Macdonald Block
900 Bay Street
Toronto, Ontario   M7A 2E5
Telephones

from Toronto:
English (416) 965-4008
Français (416) 965-3448
for recorded campground vacancy reports:
(416) 364-4722

from Canada (except Northwest Territories):
  English 1-800-268-3735
  Français 1-800-268-3736
from continental United States (except New York State):
  1-800-828-8585
from New York State:
  1-800-462-8404

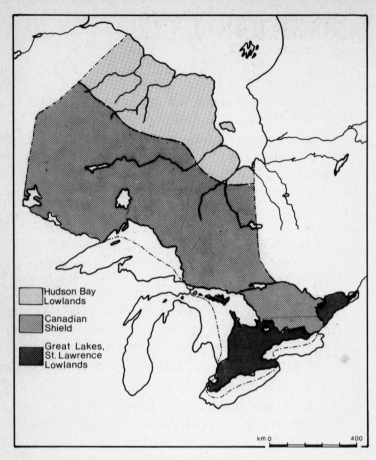

Hudson Bay
Lowlands

Canadian
Shield

Great Lakes,
St. Lawrence
Lowlands

km 0   400

The General Geographic Regions of Ontario (2)

Ontario's Trails

An Overview

When all the nature trails, fitness trails, multi-purpose trails, and other marked pathways in the province's 133 provincial parks, 304 conservation areas, 4 national parks, and hundreds of other public properties are taken into account, it quickly becomes clear that complete descriptions are far beyond the scope of this book. What follows, then, is a selection of the *best* of those hundreds of trails. Generally speaking, aside from a few shorter trails, only trails over twenty kilometres (or about one day's hiking) have been included in the detailed outlines. Hikers wanting to know more about the many other trails can contact the managing agency directly.

Trails described in detail in the following pages are divided into a number of groups based on the nature of their organization and management:

1. Trails built and maintained by volunteers (Federation of Ontario Hiking Trail Associations)
2. Provincial park and Crown Land trails
3. Conservation authority trails
4. National park trails
5. Other trails

Each trail is outlined in the following manner:

Managing Organization: The primary source of up-to-date trail information. Many organizations publish detailed maps, guidebooks, or brochures.

Location: northwestern, northeastern, eastern, central or southwestern Ontario. Trail termini and/or nearby city or town.

Length: Total hiking distance in kilometres.

Degree of Difficulty: "Easy" — few if any steep slopes or rough trailway conditions requiring special footwear or equipment. Suited to adolescents or novices for short segments or day outings. "Moderate" — longer distances. Some locally rough, wet, and steep conditions may require durable clothing and footwear. Should only be attempted by persons having a reasonable degree of fitness and health. "Challenging" — long-distance backpacking trails requiring sufficient equipment, food, and shelter for several days. Trails of this category have trailway conditions that require good physical fitness, experience, and sturdy equipment and footwear. Not to be attempted by novices or those having little experience except under the guidance and support of trained leaders.

These difficulty ratings are intended to serve solely as a guide to the general nature of the trails. Since some trails, even short ones, may have sections of any degree of difficulty, hikers must personally accept all responsibility for their own comfort and safety by properly informing themselves of detailed trail conditions before beginning any outing.

Comments: A brief description of the scenic natural beauty to be seen along the way, the general route, marking system, campsites, water sources, shelters, etc.

Volunteer Trails

The more than twenty-one hundred kilometres of hiking trails in this group were built and are maintained almost solely by volunteer members of the nine hiking clubs and associations which make up the Federation of Ontario Hiking Trail Associations (FOHTA). Some sections of trail lying within parks or conservation areas are managed at least partly by paid park or conservation authority staff, but the bulk of the trail work is done by volunteers. (Some of the "Other Trails" listed in Part 5 are also volunteer-maintained. Since they are not part of the FOHTA group and are generally not long-distance hiking trails, they are considered separately.)

Marking systems on FOHTA trails vary. The Bruce Trail has white 5 cm x 15 cm painted blazes at eye level on trees, rocks, fenceposts, stiles, etc., with blue blazes for side trails. The Guelph Trail employs orange blazes, while the Rideau Trail uses a coloured isosceles triangle. In each case the maps and/or trail guide material published by the managing organization indicates the type of blazes and signs used. Whatever the system, hikers must heed the first rule of the Trail User's Code: hike only along marked routes. Most of the volunteer trails cross private land — much of it in agricultural production. Wandering off the approved route may cause a section of the trail to be closed by the landowner, thus necessitating an unfortunate rerouting onto nearby roads.

Although the FOHTA trails are open and free for use by anyone who abides by the Trail User's Code, membership in one or more of the trail associations is strongly encouraged. Aside from the many benefits for the hiker, such as up-to-date trail information, possible discounts for club publications, and price reductions for card-carrying members at many sporting goods stores and hostels, it is only reasonable to expect that a trail user will help to support the volunteer management efforts that go into the trails.

For general information about Ontario's volunteer trails contact:

The Federation of Ontario Hiking Trail Associations
P. O. Box 422
Cambridge, Ontario   N1R 5V5

Avon Trail

Managing Organization:
The Avon Trail Association
P. O. Box 346
Stratford, Ontario   N5A 6T4

Location: southwestern Ontario, Stratford area

Length: 100 km

Degree of Difficulty: easy to moderate

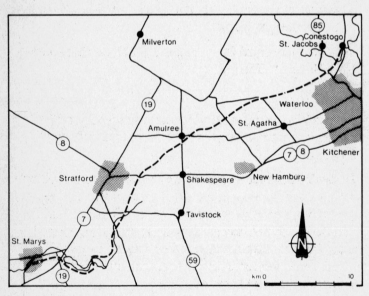

The Avon Trail (3)

Comments: The Avon Trail follows the placid Avon River through the City of Stratford, home of the world-famous Stratford Shakespearean Festival. A side loop of the trail passes the Festival Theatre.

Much of the trail, which connects with the Thames Valley Trail in the village of St. Marys and the Grand River Trail in Conestogo, runs through productive farmland.

About thirteen kilometres of trail lie within the Wildwood Conservation Area, managed by the Upper Thames River Conservation Authority.

Bruce Trail

Managing Organization:
   The Bruce Trail Association
   P. O. Box 857
   Hamilton, Ontario   L8N 3N9
   Telephone (416) 689-7311

Location: south-central Ontario, along the Niagara Escarpment from Niagara to Tobermory

Length: 700 km

Degree of Difficulty: Some local sections easy, the majority moderate, up to 100 km (mainly in Bruce Peninsula) very challenging.

Comments: The Bruce Trail was founded in 1961 and completed in 1967. It is the longest and the oldest continuous volunteer trail in Ontario and is maintained by nine local Bruce Trail clubs, most of which publish newsletters and conduct organized hikes and other outings. The seven-thousand-member association is also very active in land acquisition, public education, landowner relations, etc.

The trail, thirty-six per cent of which crosses private land,

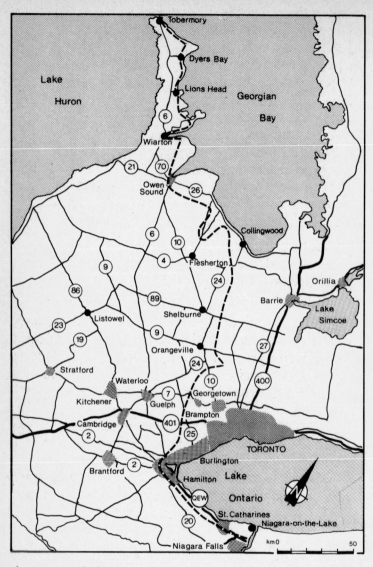

The Bruce Trail (4)

follows the scenic Niagara Escarpment — a linear complex of limestone cliffs, waterfalls, glacial valleys, and woodland — from Queenston, on the Niagara River, to Tobermory, at the tip of the Bruce Peninsula.

Many rare and beautiful ferns, orchids, and other plants found in few other locations in Ontario occur along the trail, as do white-tailed deer, coyotes, black bear, foxes, turkey vultures, Massasauga rattlesnakes, and many other species of birds and animals. And the scenery is without equal in southern Ontario!

For more information about the geology, hydrology, vegetation, wildlife, and cultural/historic aspects of the Niagara Escarpment, contact:

The Niagara Escarpment Commission
232 Guelph Street
Georgetown, Ontario   L7G 4B1
Phone: (416) 877-5191 or 453-2468 (from Toronto)

The trail is marked by 5 cm x 15 cm painted white blazes and by a standardized system of black-and-white metal signs marking access points, some thirty-five campsites and shelters, and so on. Side trails are marked with blue blazes. Abrupt changes in trail direction are marked by double blazes, one above the other.

The Bruce Trail Association publishes an excellent guidebook containing detailed coloured maps and text describing the trail and its environs. Other publications, *Cross-Country Skiing on the Bruce Trail*, a *Manual for Group Hiking on the Bruce Trail*, and an annual *Bruce Trail Calendar*, are also available.

Elgin Trail

Managing Organization:
  The Elgin Trail Club
  P. O. Box 11
  St. Thomas, Ontario   N5P 3T5

Location: southwestern Ontario, St. Thomas area

Length: 25 km

Degree of Difficulty: easy to moderate

Comments: This is the southernmost and shortest of the FOHTA trails. Being located in that part of Ontario known as the Deciduous (or Carolinian) Forest Region, the Elgin Trail offers an opportunity to see many tree species common to the eastern and southeastern United States and not found in Ontario north of the Hamilton–Sarnia latitude.

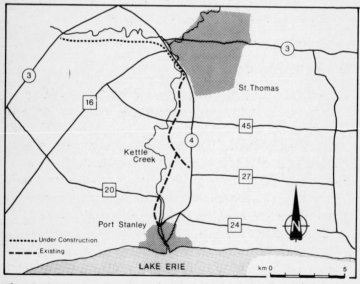

The Elgin Trail (5)

The trail generally follows the Kettle Creek valley from St. Thomas to Port Stanley, on the shore of Lake Erie. Actually, it is in two sections: the first, from St. Thomas to Highway #4, just north of Union, is marked by white blazes; the second, from that area south to Port Stanley, is a side trail marked by blue blazes. A third section is presently being constructed from St. Thomas northwest to Paynes Mills on Highway #3, along the Dodds Creek valley.

Ganaraska Trail

Managing Organization:
    The Ganaraska Trail Association
    P. O. Box 1136
    Barrie, Ontario   L4M 5E2

Location: south-central Ontario, Port Hope to Devil's Glen (near Collingwood) via Orillia, Midland, and Barrie

Length: 200 km

Degree of Difficulty: moderate

Comments: The Ganaraska Trail, which connects in two places with the Bruce Trail south of Collingwood, is an excellent way to explore the varied landscape and colourful history of north Simcoe County and the beautiful scenery of the Ganaraska highlands east of Lake Simcoe. This is Huronia, the land of Samuel de Champlain and the Jesuit missionaries of the 1600s, and of the Huron Indians who lived in the area for several centuries before the arrival of the white man. Numerous archaeological and historical sites are located along the trail.

Although still under development, three major sections managed by two local trail clubs are available from Port Hope, on the shore of Lake Ontario, north to Omemee, near

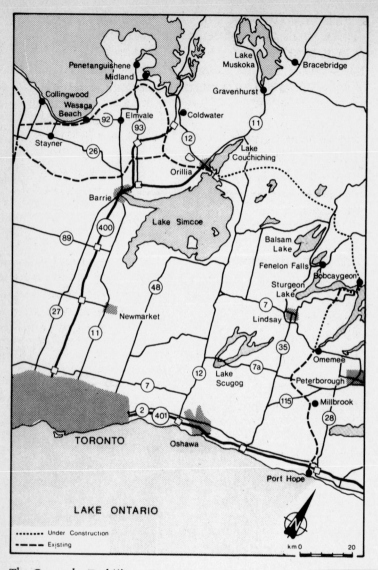

The Ganaraska Trail (6)

Peterborough. The second and third actually form a loop, with one branch running east from Devil's Glen Provincial Park through Angus, skirting the edge of the Minesing Swamp — rich in flora and fauna — north and west of the city of Barrie and eastward through the sandhills of the Simcoe Uplands. The other branch runs east from Duntroon through Wasaga Beach before swinging west and south past the Great Lakes port towns of Midland, Port McNicol, and Victoria Harbour to complete the loop just west of Orillia.

Between Rama (near Orillia) and Omemee the trail, with the exception of a small section south of Bobcaygeon, is still in planning and construction stages.

There are no campsites or shelters on the trail as yet. However, camping is available at nearby Devil's Glen Provincial Park, Bass Lake Provincial Park, and Emily Provincial Park, as well as at a number of commercial campgrounds in the area.

The Ganaraska Trail is marked by white painted blazes and brown-and-white logo signs. The Ganaraska Trail Association publishes an excellent guidebook containing maps and trail notes.

Grand Valley Trail

Managing Organization:
  The Grand Valley Trails Association
  P. O. Box 1233
  Kitchener, Ontario   N2G 4G8

Location: southwestern Ontario, Kitchener area

Length: 125 km

Degree of Difficulty: easy to moderate

Comments: The Grand Valley Trail generally follows the valley of the Grand River from the city of Brantford north through

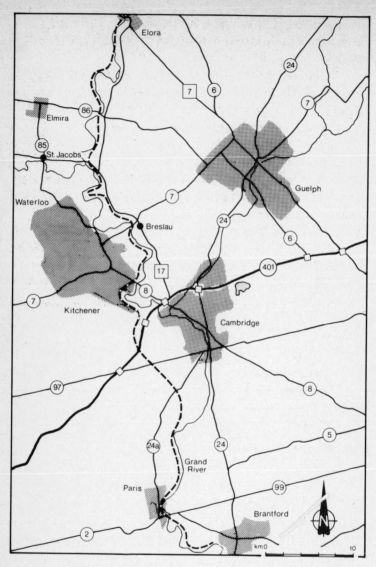

The Grand Valley Trail (7)

Paris, Cambridge, Kitchener, Waterloo, Conestogo (where it connects with the Avon Trail), and on to Elora, just west of Fergus.

This is a prosperous, long-established farming area with many active farms still in the hands of the descendants of the original Mennonite and Pennsylvania Dutch families.

The trail is marked with white painted blazes with blue-blazed side trails.

Although there is no camping directly along the trail, camping is available at a number of nearby cconservation areas (e.g., Brant, Pinehurst Lake, Elora Gorge) operated by the Grand River Conservation Authority. Contact the Authority directly for information on camping. (See Appendix 3)

The Grand Valley Trail Association publishes detailed maps of the trail route.

Guelph & Speed River Trails

Managing Organization:
 Guelph Trail Club
 P. O. Box 1
 Guelph, Ontario   N1H 6J6

Location: southwestern Ontario, Guelph area

Length: 65 km

Degree of Difficulty: easy to moderate

Comments: The Guelph Trail Club manages these two trails, both marked with painted orange blazes. The Guelph Radial Trail follows the abandoned bed of an historic railway east from the city, along the Eramosa River valley past Blue Springs and the hamlet of Eden Mills to a point just north of the village of Limehouse, where it joins the Bruce Trail. Along the way, it passes through some very pleasant, rolling landscape (shaped

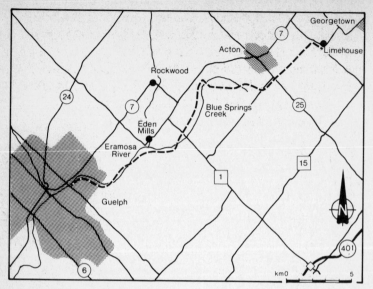

The Guelph Radial Trail (8)

by glaciers over nine thousand years ago) containing several excellent examples of *eskers* (long, snaking gravel ridges), jumbled gravel hills called *drumlins*, and low spring-fed cedar bogs.

There are no campsites along the trail, however, camping is available at the Rockwood Conservation Area on Highway #7, some three kilometres north of the trail via the fourth line road or the Guelph Line. The camp area is managed by the Grand River Conservation Authority.

The Speed River Trail runs west from the city of Guelph, along the Speed River valley to the town of Preston. The landscape along this trail offers a similar opportunity to see and study glacial landforms. There is no camping along the trail.

Although there is no blazed path through the city of Guelph, a system of linear riverside parks allows for pleasant walking through a very attractive urban setting characterised by many fine historic buildings built of local limestone.

Two loop trails totalling twelve kilometres extend to the

south of the Guelph Radial Trail east of the city and another six-kilometre loop provides access to conservation authority lands in the Hanlon Creek watershed west of the city. The area is rich in flora and fauna and is designated an Environmentally Sensitive Area — hikers must stay on the marked route.

The Guelph Trail Club publishes a very useful and easy-to-read guide to all of the above trails.

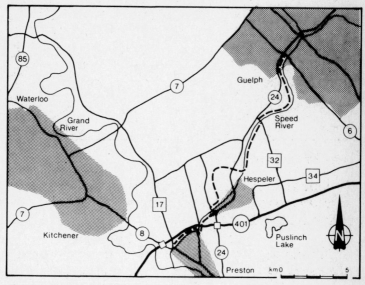

The Speed River Trail (9)

Rideau Trail

Managing Organization:
   The Rideau Trail Organization
   P. O. Box 15
   Kingston, Ontario   K7L 4V6

Location: eastern Ontario. Kingston to Ottawa along the Rideau River and Canal

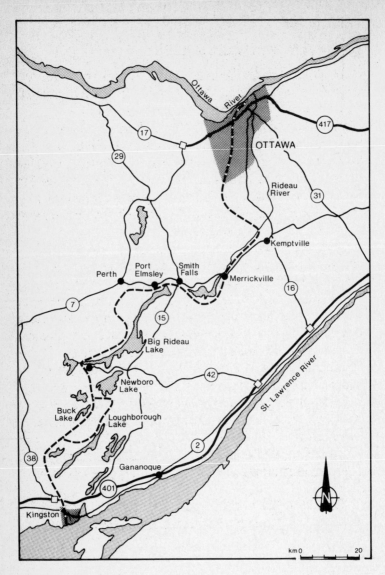

The Rideau Trail (10)

Length: 386 km

Degree of Difficulty: moderate to challenging

Comments: For decades, boaters have known the scenic beauty to be found along the route of the historic Rideau Canal, built by Colonel John By between 1826 and 1832 as a route for transporting military supplies and men between Bytown (Ottawa) and Kingston. In 1971 a volunteer committee, along with a group of students working under an Opportunities for Youth grant, completed the construction of the entire 386-km Rideau Hiking Trail in less than six months! Now, hikers can walk through these scenic and historic lands, following many kilometres of the Rideau Canal itself.

This area of eastern Ontario is a geologically and ecologically interesting one. A complex juxtaposition of Paleozoic and Pre-Cambrian rock, sculpted by glaciers some ten thousand years ago, has produced a varied landscape of coniferous and deciduous forest, bogs, limestone plains, rolling granitic ridges, lakes, and streams. The trail runs through and near several provincial parks, conservation areas, and commercial campgrounds as well as several campgrounds maintained by the Rideau Trail Association. Limited camping is also available for card-carrying members of the Rideau Trail Association on federal lands adjacent to several locks on the Rideau Canal.

The Association has published a series of detailed maps and a very informative book, *Rideau Trail Notes: A Companion to the Map Kit.*

The Rideau Trail is highly recommended to anyone who wishes to experience the real character of eastern Ontario.

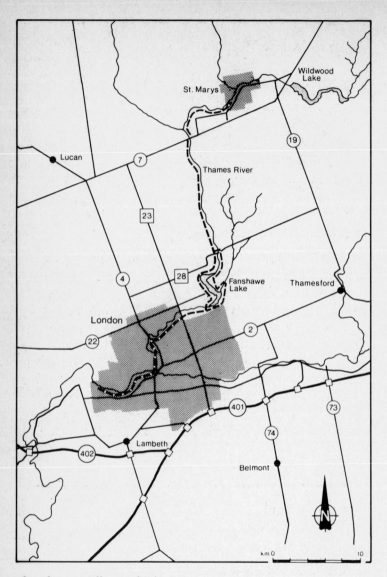

The Thames Valley Trail (11)

Thames Valley Trail

Managing Organization:
  The Thames Valley Trail Association
  P. O. Box 821
  Terminal "B"
  London, Ontario   N6A 4Z3

Location: southwestern Ontario. London to St. Marys

Length: 56 km

Degree of Difficulty: easy to moderate

Comments: The Thames Valley Trail is a pleasant route up the valley of the Thames River, starting in Springbank Park in the southwest area of the city of London, passing through the campus of the University of Western Ontario, and turning north through farmland to the village of St. Marys, where it joins the Avon Trail. Most of the trail is on private land.

The trailway is marked by white blazes and Thames Valley Trail Association green-and-white logo signs. Although there is no camping on the trail, group campsites are available at the Fanshawe Conservation Area. Contact the Upper Thames Region Conservation Authority for details. (See Appendix 3)

Voyageur Trail

Managing Organization:
  The Voyageur Trail Association
  P. O. Box 66
  Sault Ste. Marie, Ontario   P6A 5L2

Location: northern Ontario. Manitoulin Island to Thunder Bay

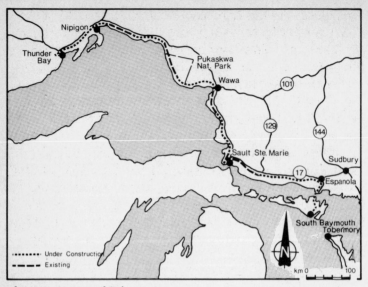

The Voyageur Trail (12)

Length: 350 km (completed to date)

Degree of Difficulty: moderate to very challenging.

Comments: When completed, the Voyageur Trail will be the longest, most rugged, and most scenic trail in Ontario. Even now, the approximately 350 km that have been completed (with some clearing and marking still needed in places) offer some very challenging wilderness hiking.

The southern terminus of the trail is in the village of South Baymouth, just an hour and three-quarters ride on the modern car-ferry M.S. *Chi Cheemaun* from Tobermory, the northern terminus of the Bruce Trail. From South Baymouth the route winds north across the east end of Manitoulin Island to Little Current, where it crosses to the mainland and enters "Rainbow Country," south of the pulp and paper town of Espanola. In this area the white quartzite La Cloche Mountains (the same range that passes through Killarney Provincial Park) combined with the azure blue skies and lakes and rich green conifers make for some truly magnificent scenery.

The route follows the north shore of Lake Huron west from Espanola to Sault Ste. Marie, where it swings north along the shore of Lake Superior, the largest, deepest, and coldest of the Great Lakes. In this area, a number of discontinuous sections have been completed but much work remains to be done.

Hikers wishing to try the Voyageur Trail, especially the northernmost sections, are strongly advised to check with the Voyageur Trail Association for up-to-date trail information. Also, because of the ruggedness and remoteness of the area along the Lake Superior shoreline, hikers should not attempt a trip unless they are experienced, in good physical condition, and have good equipment. Leaving word of the route and approximate hiking schedule with someone would be wise as well, as it is for any wilderness outing.

The Lake Superior shoreline offers some of the most breathtaking scenery in Ontario — a fact recognized by several artists of the Group of Seven — but part of that splendour involves the Lake's notorious weather.

In good weather or bad, though, there is nothing to beat the rocky cliffs, secluded beaches and coves, and rushing rivers, many of which are choked with migrating salmon in the autumn. The ancient Indian pictographs at Agawa Rock are famous among tourists willing to trek the short distance from the nearest road in Lake Superior Provincial Park, but they are only one of several exciting discoveries that await the through-hiker. A camera and plenty of film are musts — especially in the autumn.

The Voyageur Trail is marked by painted white blazes (with blue blazes for side trails) and blue-and-yellow metal logo signs. Campsites, access points, water sources, etc. are shown in a detailed guidebook published by the Voyageur Trail Association.

Hiking and nature trails are ideal for use not just by hikers, but by school groups, naturalists' clubs, Scouts and Guides, and many other organizations.

Provincial Park Trails

Almost every one of Ontario's 133 provincial parks contains trail systems of some length. The majority tend to be short (less than three kilometres) nature-interpretation trails that invite the visitor to explore a particular aspect of the landscape, perhaps beaver pond or bog ecology, geology, pioneer history, or simply some of the most scenic views east of the Rockies. Such trails should not be ignored by the long-distance hiker, as they can make excellent warm-up trips and serve as good introductions to the kinds of things that may be encountered on longer trails in the same area. Similarly, novices, adolescents, and some handicapped persons unable to tackle long expeditions will find such interpretive trails ideal.

North of a line from Parry Sound to Kingston, over eighty per cent of the land is in the public domain, known as Crown Lands. In these areas, hundreds of kilometres of forest access roads and snowmobile and cross-country ski trails have been established. Many such routes — too many to list or map here — are multi-purpose trails not specifically designed or perhaps even marked for hiking. They nevertheless provide some excellent wilderness travel opportunities to those with the experience and equipment, especially good maps and compass.

Anyone wishing to venture into such areas should contact the District or Regional offices of the Ministry of Natural Resources to determine any access restrictions due to fire danger, private lease areas, etc.

A selection of seventeen major long-distance trails in the provincial park and Crown Land systems follows. As on the volunteer trails, route-marking symbols may vary somewhat from trail to trail. Generally speaking, however, trails are well marked and maintained and should not be difficult to follow.

Each trail is described in detail in maps and brochures provided by the respective park offices.

Ontario's provincial parks are open (that is, services are provided) for varying periods from May to October, depending on the park. Hikers should inquire about operation times, and about entry and permit fees as part of their trip planning. Hiking during off-season should not be discounted; there are fewer bugs and people!

Algonquin Provincial Park

Western Uplands Hiking Trail

Managing Organization:
    Ministry of Natural Resources
    Algonquin Provincial Park,
    P. O. Box 219
    Whitney, Ontario   KoJ 2Mo
    Telephone (705) 633-5572

Location: central Ontario. 45 km east of Huntsville on Highway #60

Length: 90 km

Degree of Difficulty: challenging

Comments: This trail, located in the western part of the park, is composed of a series of sequential loops. This allows the hiker to choose any length of trip that time and ability permit.

The trail follows rolling well-treed terrain along rocky ridges and hills separated by streams and bogs. Depending on the weather and time of the year, hikers will likely see or hear signs of moose, white-tailed deer, timber wolf, common loon, and many other species of birds and animals.

The trail and over seventy primitive campsites are well marked and the park publication *Hiking Trails for Back Packers*, is very useful and easy to follow.

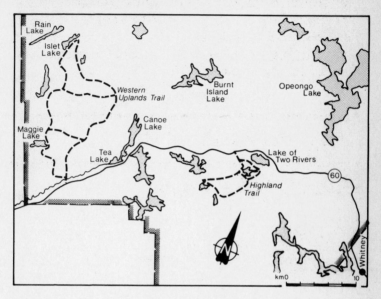

The Western Uplands Trail and the Highland Trail, both in Algonquin Provincial Park (13)

Algonquin Provincial Park

Highland Hiking Trail

Managing Organization:
Ministry of Natural Resources
Algonquin Provincial Park
P. O. Box 219
Whitney, Ontario KoJ 2Mo
Telephone (705) 633-5572

A *beaver pond and meadow in* Algonquin Provincial Park.

Location: central Ontario. 73 km east of Huntsville on Highway #60.

Length: 35 km

Degree of Difficulty: challenging

Comments: Although shorter than the Western Upland Trail, the Highland Trail is equally challenging, providing a good opportunity for two to three days of back-country hiking through some beautiful Algonquin landscape, especially in the autumn. Over twenty primitive campsites have been designated along the trail's two major loops.

Rules & Regulations: On both of the above trails, hikers must camp only in the designated campsites and leave no trace when moving out in the morning. For example, no vegetation may be cut for bedding, surrounding trees must not be damaged, and litter, cans, or bottles must not be left behind. Party size is limited to nine per designated campsite and interior camping permits must be obtained before starting any overnight hike. During busy seasons, however, the total number of hikers allowed onto the trails is limited. Hikers should be prepared for an unexpected delay or change in plans if the "first-come-first-served" quota has been reached before their arrival.

Bon Echo Provincial Park

Abes & Essens Lakes Hiking Trail

Managing Organization:
Ministry of Natural Resources
Bon Echo Provincial Park
R. R. #1
Cloyne, Ontario   K0H 1K0
Telephone (613) 336-2228

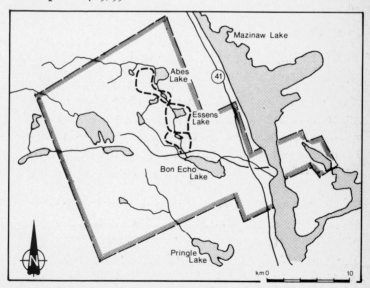

The Abes and Essens Lakes Trail in Bon Echo Provincial Park (14)

Location: eastern Ontario. 80 km north of Napanee on Highway #41

Length: 31 km

Degree of Difficulty: moderate

Comments: This trail is similar in layout to the Western Uplands Hiking Trail in Algonquin Park in that it is composed of a "stacked" series of three loops approximately four, ten, and seventeen kilometres long. The geology, topography, forest cover, and wildlife are also not too different from those found in Algonquin. Bon Echo Provincial Park does have its own character, however, and is well worth exploring via this trail system.

Five primitive campsites are situated along the shores of Abes and Essens lakes and interior permits (available at the park gate) are required.

Esker Lakes Provincial Park

Trapper's Hiking Trail

Managing Organization:
Ministry of Natural Resources
Esker Lakes Provincial Park
P. O. Box 129
Swastika, Ontario   P0K 1T0
Telephone (705) 567-4849

Location: northeastern Ontario. Northeast of Kirkland Lake

Length: 20 km

Degree of Difficulty: moderate

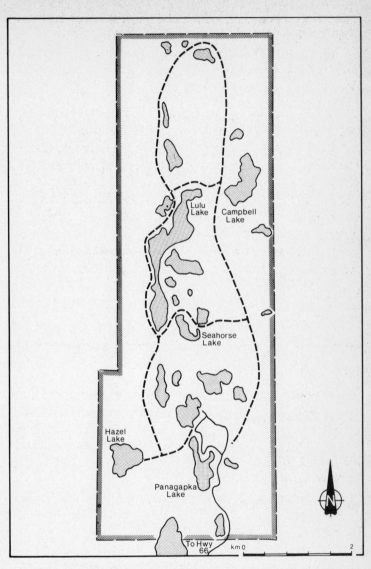

The Trapper's Hiking Trail in Esker Lakes Provincial Park (15)

Comments: Although this trail might be covered in a day, the fascinating geology and history of the area demand that more time be taken. While many of Ontario's trails provide good access to other examples of the post-glacial landforms of the province, the trail system of Esker Lakes Provincial Park is one of the best.

The trail also passes through forest that has been subjected to intermittent forest fires during the past fifty years — a fascinating study in forest ecology. This is a part of the province where, not so long ago, fur trapping was a major part of the regional economy. Mining, particularly for gold, began during the early 1900s and remains an important activity in the area.

Frontenac Provincial Park

Frontenac Park Trail System

Managing Organization:
   Ministry of Natural Resources
   Frontenac Provincial Park
   1 Richmond Blvd.
   Napanee, Ontario   K7R 3S3
   Telephone (613) 354-2173

Location: eastern Ontario. 30 km north of Kingston.

Length: 100 km

Degree of Difficulty: moderate to challenging

Comments: Frontenac Provincial Park is a new park; parts of it are still in the planning and development stages. Much has been done, however, and over a hundred kilometres of trails are now available for use.

This area is part of the same geologist's paradise alluded to

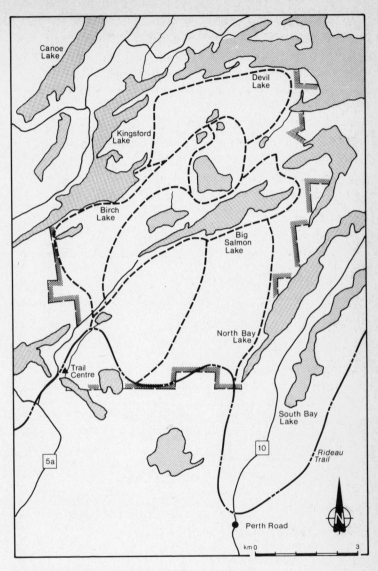

The Frontenac Provincial Park Trail System (16)

in the description of the Rideau Trail. The Rideau Trail is incorporated into the southern part of the Frontenac Park Trail system, which forms a network pattern, no part of which is more than twelve kilometres from the Trail Centre.

Camping permits must be obtained at the Trail Centre. Group size is limited to six persons per campsite. There are eleven campsite clusters, each with four campsites, in the park interior. Each cluster has picnic tables, privy toilets, and some fire pits.

This is an excellent trail system for through-hikers on the Rideau Trail, or for those who wish to explore Frontenac Park itself.

Halfway Lake Provincial Park

Hawk Ridge Trail

Managing Organization:
    Ministry of Natural Resources
    Halfway Lake Provincial Park
    P. O. Box 3500
    Station "A"
    Sudbury, Ontario P3A 4S2
    Telephone (705) 522-7823
    Park phone (705) 965-2702

Location: northern Ontario. 90 km northwest of Sudbury on Highway #144

Length: 30 km

Degree of Difficulty: moderate to challenging

Comments: This trail provides a two- to three-day backpacking trip through rolling mixed coniferous and deciduous bush.

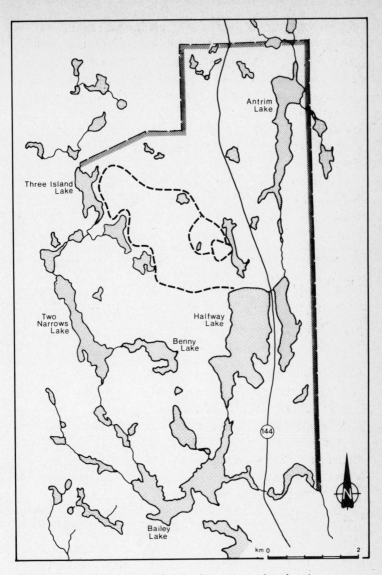

The Hawk Ridge Trail in Halfway Lake Provincial Park (17)

The western part of the thirty-kilometre loop follows a chain of very pretty wilderness lakes. Wonderful sunsets may be enjoyed from a number of lookouts along the way.

As with all other park trails, hikers should camp at designated campsites and register at the park gate before starting out.

Killarney Provincial Park

Baie Fine Trail

Managing Organization:
    Ministry of Natural Resources
    Killarney Provincial Park
    Killarney, Ontario   P0M 2A0
    Telephone (705) 287-2368

Location: central Ontario. 50 km southwest of Sudbury

Length: 13 km linear (26 km return trip)

Degree of Difficulty: very challenging

Comments: Killarney Provincial Park is unofficially known as the crown jewel of Ontario's provincial park system. After a few days' hiking amid the snow-white quartzite ridges, crystal clear lakes, and blue skies of the La Cloche Mountains area, the reasons for this title become quite obvious.

The Baie Fine Trail, the slightly less challenging of Killarney's two hiking trails, follows this up-and-down terrain past the west end of George Lake and a number of smaller lakes to a point at the northwest end of Threenarrows Lake. Baie Fine, a popular fjord-like shelter for sailboats cruising the Georgian Bay—North Channel area, is a little over halfway along the trail.

A half dozen primitive campsites are scattered along the thirteen-kilometre route.

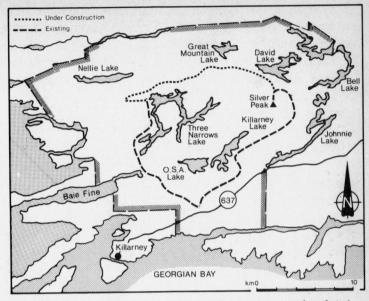

The Silver Peak and Baie Fine trails, in Killarney Provincial Park (18)

Killarney Provincial Park

Silver Peak Trail

Managing Organization:
Ministry of Natural Resources
Killarney Provincial Park
Killarney, Ontario   P0M 2A0
Telephone (705) 207-2368

Location: central Ontario. 50 km southwest of Sudbury

Length: 35 km linear (70 km return trip)

Degree of Difficulty: very challenging

Comments: Unlike the rolling trailways of many southern trails, the Silver Peak Trail climbs over three hundred and fifty metres of elevation along and over ridge backs and streams and around beaver meadows to the top of Silver Peak (543 m above sea level). From the tops of many of these ridges the view on a clear day can be breathtaking: over fifty kilometres to the south down the rocky and wild Georgian Bay coastline, or westward toward "Rainbow Country" lying north of Manitoulin Island (see the Voyageur Trail).

In addition to sites at the developed George Lake campground, there are almost a dozen primitive designated campsites along the trail, which is blazed by blue diamond markers.

Ultimately it is intended to link the Silver Peak and Baie Fine trails to form a loop about a hundred kilometres in length (ten to fourteen days hiking) across the north ridges of the La Cloche Mountains. Until then, either of the two trails is well worth the trip.

An excellent plasticised paper map showing canoe portages and trails and other useful information is available for a price from the Ministry of Natural Resources Public Service Centre in Toronto or from their Killarney Park office.

Rules and Regulations: Killarney Provincial Park is one of the most environmentally sensitive parks in Ontario. For this reason hikers should take extra care to leave no trace of their visit behind them when they move on, camping only in designated campsites, cutting no vegetation, and leaving no cans or bottles. Group size must be kept small and all hikers must obtain interior permits on a first-come-first-served basis through the Park's "Visitor Distribution Program." As Killarney is a popular park, "off-season" hiking during the spring or fall or hiking on weekdays rather than on long weekends might be a good idea.

Lake Superior Provincial Park

Coastal Trail

Managing Organization:
    Ministry of Natural Resources
    Lake Superior Provincial Park
    P. O. Box 1160
    Wawa, Ontario   P0S 1K0
    Telephone (705) 856-2284

Location: northern Ontario. 140 km north of Sault Ste. Marie on Highway #17

Length: 40 km

Degree of Difficulty: very challenging

A beach in the Coldwater River area, part of Lake Superior Provincial Park traversed by the Coastal Trail.

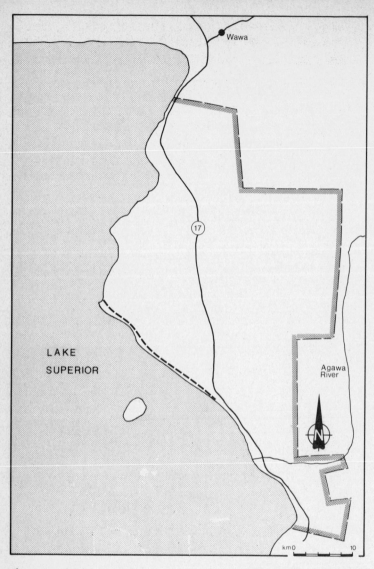

The Coastal Trail in Lake Superior Provincial Park (19)

Comments: At this point in the development of hiking trails within Lake Superior Provincial Park, the Coastal Trail is the longest and most rugged of the park's trails. It follows the wild and beautiful shoreline of Lake Superior from Coldwater Creek to Indian Harbour. Along the way the hiker will experience a pristine landscape steeped in Ojibway Indian legends.

As advised in the section on the Voyageur Trail (which, it is hoped, will eventually follow the Coastal Trail route through and beyond the park) this trail requires a high degree of physical fitness, planning, experience, and good equipment. Weather conditions in this area are unpredictable and can be very dangerous.

There are four other hiking trails in the park. The first three — the Orphan Lake Trail, an eleven-kilometre loop; the Peat Mountain Trail, a sixteen-kilometre loop; and the Awausee Lookout Trail, also a sixteen-kilometre loop — may be hiked in one day each. The fourth, the Towabanasay Trail, is a linear trail of thirty-three kilometres return.

A campsite is located at Burnt Rock Pool, near the eastern end of the Towabanasay Trail.

Quetico Provincial Park

Abandoned Tote Road System

Managing Organization:
　　Ministry of Natural Resources
　　Quetico Provincial Park
　　Atikokan, Ontario　　P0T 1C0
　　Telephone (807) 597-2735

Location: northwestern Ontario. Northeast section of Quetico Provincial Park

Length: 100 km

Degree of Difficulty: moderate

Comments: This trail system is composed of a network of abandoned logging roads in the area of Zephira, McKenzie, Cache, Trousers, and Baptism lakes. The roads have been abandoned for many years and for the most part have been reclaimed by the forest. This profusion of new growth coupled with the remoteness of the area, have made for relatively high populations of timber wolf and moose.

Quetico Provincial Park

Howard Lake Hiking Trail

Managing Organization:
    Ministry of Natural Resources
    Quetico Provincial Park
    Atikokan, Ontario   P0T 1C0
    Telephone (807) 597-2735

Location: northwestern Ontario. 160 km west of Thunder Bay on Highway #11. Access via Dawson Trail Campground.

Length: 28 km loop

Degree of Difficulty: moderate to challenging

Comments: This is a trail of the northern boreal forests. In the western portion, black spruce forests edging sphagnum bogs alternate with rock ridges rimmed with jack pine stands. Howard Lake offers good northern pike fishing. The eastern part of the trail passes through areas disturbed by logging in the mid 1970s. In these areas timber wolves, moose, and black bear are frequently seen.

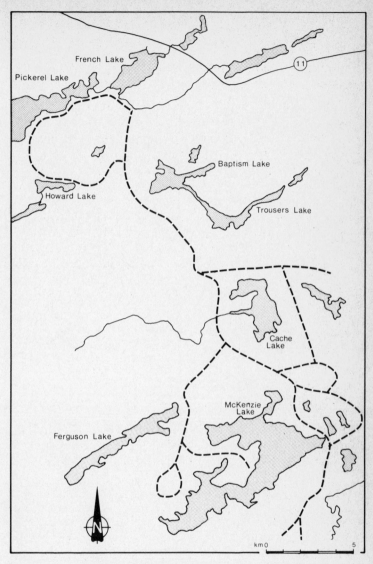

The Howard Lake Hiking Trail and the Abandoned Tote Road
System, both in Quetico Provincial Park (20)

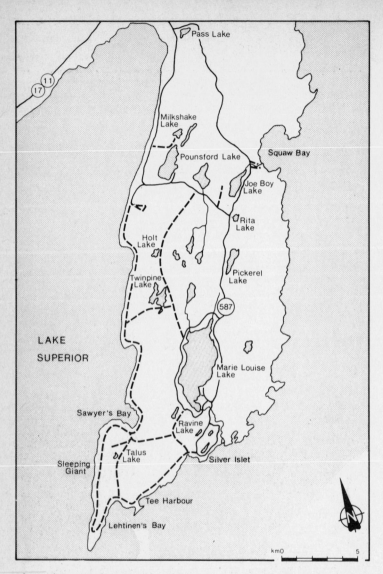

The Kabeyun Hiking Trail in Sibley Provincial Park (21)

Kabeyun Hiking Trail

Managing Organization:
   Ministry of Natural Resources
   Thunder Bay District
   P. O. Box 5000
   435 James Street South
   Thunder Bay, Ontario   P7C 5G6
   Telephone (807) 475-1531

Location: northwestern Ontario, Thunder Bay area

Length: 40 km

Degree of Difficulty: challenging

Comments: The Sibley Peninsula is a scenic area renowned for the "Sleeping Giant" rock formation, visible from Thunder Bay

The figure of the Sleeping Giant dominates Sibley Provincial Park.

some twenty-five kilometres to the west. The views from atop the park's soaring cliffs and ridges, which rise two hundred fifty metres above the waters of Lake Superior, are spectacular.

The Kabeyun Trail, the longest of the hiking trails in the park, can provide for two to three days of hiking and camping in a rugged wilderness setting — much more if time is taken to explore all that the park has to offer. In addition to the Kabeyun Trail, which runs down the west side of the peninsula, there are almost forty-five kilometres of other trails in the park, making for a total of eighty-five kilometres; a great part of Ontario's northland in which to spend a week or more!

Access to the park is via Highway #587 from Highway #17 about thirty kilometres east of the city of Thunder Bay.

Wakami Lake Provincial Park

The Height of Land Hiking Trail

Managing Organization:
    Ministry of Natural Resources
    Wakami Lake Provincial Park
    34 Birch Street
    Chapleau, Ontario   P0M 1K0
    Telephone (705) 864-1710

Location: northern Ontario. Approximately 150 km northeast of Sault Ste. Marie

Length: 75 km

Degree of Difficulty: moderate to challenging

Comments: This trail, named because it runs along part of the

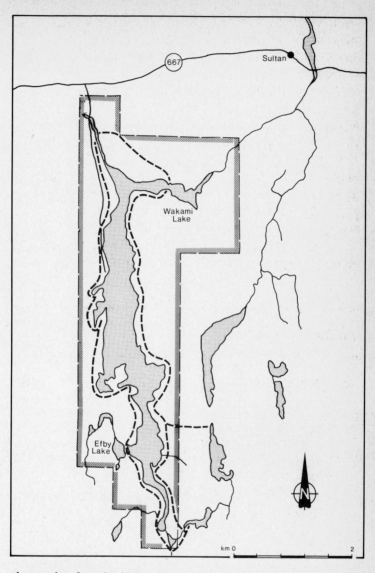

The Height of Land Hiking Trail in Wakami Lake Provincial Park (22)

height of land dividing the Hudson Bay and Great Lakes watersheds, offers a very good opportunity to hike the zone between the northern boreal and southern Great Lakes – St. Lawrence forest regions. The park is located in a relatively remote part of the province and crowding during much of the year should therefore be minimal.

Hikers should be able to see many species of wildlife along the trail, including osprey, bald eagle, merlin, hawk owl, moose, and bear. Fishing is good at many points around the shore of Wakami Lake.

All hikers should register at the park gate as a boat crossing is required on the last section of the trail. A key to unlock the boat is available from park staff.

The trail follows the shore of Wakami Lake past numerous lookouts and several relics of the area's logging history. There are twenty primitive campsites along the seventy-five kilometre loop.

Crown Land Trails

Following are four examples of the many multi-purpose trails located on Crown Land outside the provincial parks system. Because, with the exception of the Pigeon River Hiking Trail, they are multi-purpose (i.e., used for hiking, snowshoeing, cross-country skiing, snowmobiling, etc.), such trails are not designed or maintained for any one type of use and therefore some compromises — for example, easy routing versus a scenic lookout — may have to be tolerated.

Camping is allowed anywhere on the Crown Land traversed by the trails. However, hikers will probably want to stop at any of a number of sites that have become established through popular use over the years. As at any campsites, hikers should take great care with fire and leave no evidence of their presence when they break camp.

Pakkotinna Recreational Trail

Managing Organization:
    Ministry of Natural Resources
    Pembroke District
    P. O. Box 220
    Pembroke, Ontario   K8A 6X4
    Telephone (613) 732-3661

Location: eastern Ontario. 24 km west of Pembroke

Length: 40 km

Degree of Difficulty: moderate

Comments: Although designed and maintained as a snowmobile trail, the Pakkotinna Trail, which follows old logging roads and trails, can be used by hikers during the spring, summer, and fall.

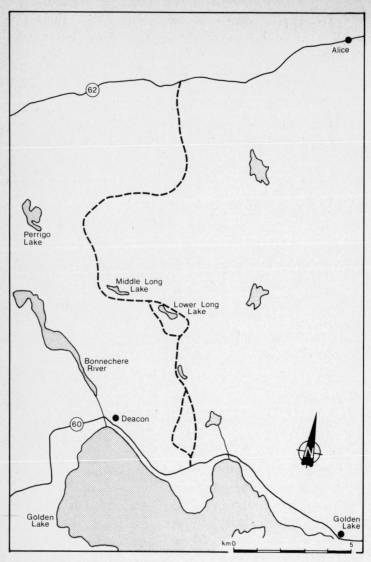

The Pakkotinna Recreational Trail, near Pembroke (23)

Access to the trail may be gained at its southern end from a parking lot on Highway #60 about eight kilometres west of Golden Lake. At its northern end, access may be gained from a similar parking lot on Highway #62 about twenty-four kilometres west of Pembroke.

Hikers should check with the district Ministry of Natural Resources office before setting out, to obtain up-to-date information on trail conditions, fire regulations, etc.

Pigeon River Hiking Trail

Managing Organization:
Ministry of Natural Resources
Thunder Bay District
P. O. Box 5000
435 James Street South
Thunder Bay, Ontario   P7G 5G6
Telephone (807) 475-1531

Location: northwestern Ontario. 75 km west of Thunder Bay on Highway #593

Length: 11 km linear (22 km return)

Degree of Difficulty: challenging

Comments: During the late 1600s and early 1700s this area was an important link in the long canoe route used by French explorers and later by the voyageurs engaged in the fur trade between Montreal and the West. The stretch of the river followed by the Pigeon River Trail was, however, too dangerous for navigation by canoe, and necessitated a major detour and numerous portages.

Although the trail is relatively short, it does provide a good one to two days of hiking along steep gorges, past rapids, and through deep forest, now recovering from several decades of

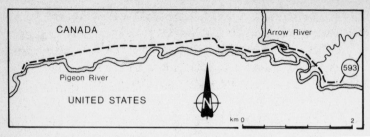

The Pigeon River Hiking Trail, west of Thunder Bay (24)

logging. It ends at the Cascades, a spectacular series of six waterfalls in a gorge thirty to forty metres deep.

Several primitive campsites are located along the trail and above the first falls.

Cars can be parked at the start of the trail at a sign marking the spot near the old international border crossing on Highway #593.

Seguin Trail

Managing Organization:
    Ministry of Natural Resources
    Parry Sound District
    4 Miller Street
    Parry Sound, Ontario   P2A 1S8
    Telephone (705) 746-4201

Location: central Ontario. Highway #69 (12 km south of Parry Sound) to Fern Glen

Length: 62 km

Degree of Difficulty: easy

Comments: This trail is unmarked, as it follows the bed of the old Ottawa, Arnprior and Parry Sound Railway, which saw active use during the early part of the century when the area was logged. Communities in the Parry Sound region enjoyed a booming trade in lumber at that time.

With some armchair research in advance this trail offers an excellent opportunity to explore a colourful period of Ontario's frontier history — a time when forest resources seemed inexhaustible.

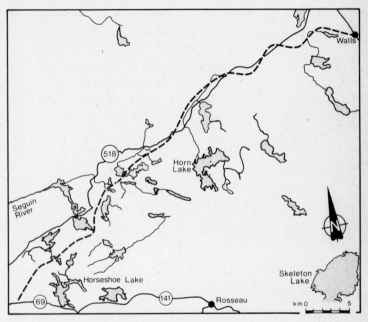

The Seguin Trail, near Parry Sound (25)

Shawanaga Trail

Managing Organization:
    Ministry of Natural Resources
    Parry Sound District
    4 Miller Street
    Parry Sound, Ontario   P2A 1S8
    Telephone (705) 746-4201

Location: central Ontario, Pointe au Baril to Ardbeg

Length: 52 km

Degree of Difficulty: moderate

Comments: This is a good trail for exploring the lichen-encrusted granite and gneiss ridges that characterise the Grenville province of Ontario's shield geology. Part of the trail also passes through a major deer yard where substantial numbers of deer congregate in winter. The trail is marked with coloured discs and wood blocks painted with fluorescent paint. It generally follows the route of an old telephone line linking fire towers in the area. The line and towers have now been replaced by radios and aircraft for forest fire prevention.

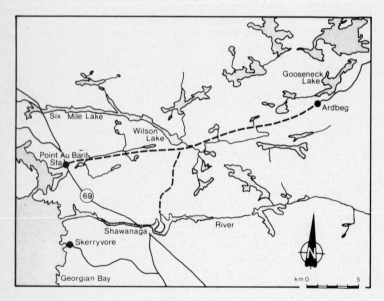

The Shawanaga Trail, west of Georgian Bay (26)

Conservation Authority Trails

Ontario's thirty-nine conservation authorities are autonomous organizations with jurisdictions based on watersheds rather than on political boundaries. Although originally formed to carry out erosion and flood control work in partnership with local municipalities and the Ontario government, most authorities also provide much-needed conservation education and outdoor recreation services to the public.

Of the 304 conservation areas in Ontario (all but 17 of which are located in southern and eastern Ontario), some 168 contain trail systems of one kind or another. Because of the limited size of most conservation areas, no trails can be classified as long-distance backpacking trails. Many do, however, allow for many hours of hiking and rambling pleasure. Such trails, short as they may be, serve a crucial role in providing public education and access to remnant natural areas.

Also, most trail systems do double duty as cross-country ski and snowshoe trails in the winter. Wherever trails are located, most conservation areas have camping facilities available. Entry and camping fees, seasons and hours of operation, and perhaps car parking fees for day users, vary from area to area, so hikers should check with authority offices well before any outing. (See Appendix 3.)

The following is a selection of five of the longer trail systems in Ontario's conservation areas. Though the selection is necessarily small, it will serve to show the kinds of trail facilities available in these areas.

Albion Hills Trails

Managing Organization:
Metropolitan Toronto and Region Conservation Authority
5 Shoreham Drive
Downsview, Ontario   M3N 1S4
Telephone (416) 661-6600

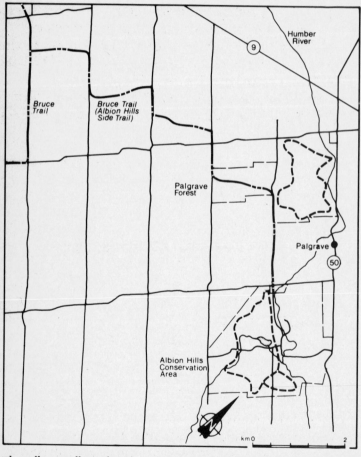

The Albion Hills Trails (27)

Location: southern Ontario. 20 km northwest of Toronto on Highway #50

Length: 20 km

Degree of Difficulty: easy

Comments: The Albion Hills Conservation Area is one of sixteen areas operated by the Metropolitan Toronto and Region Conservation Authority in the Toronto region. Located in the rolling Caledon Hills, Albion Hills Conservation Area is a popular recreational spot at all times of the year. From May to September a campground is operated at the property for hikers and visitors, who have a choice of driving in or hiking in from the Bruce Trail via an eleven-kilometre side trail from the Glen Haffy Conservation Area near Mono Mills.

The Albion Hills trails offer a good introduction to nature and hiking trails for those not ready to try a long-distance hike.

Crystal Creek Trails

Managing Organization:
    Sault Ste. Marie Region Conservation Authority
       Civic Centre
    99 Foster Drive
    Sault Ste. Marie, Ontario   P6A 5X6
    Telephone (705) 949-9111

Location: northern Ontario. Sault Ste. Marie area

Length: 35 km

Degree of Difficulty: moderate

Comments: This trail system on the northwest outskirts of the city of Sault Ste. Marie is a hiking system in summer and a groomed cross-country ski system in winter. It serves both

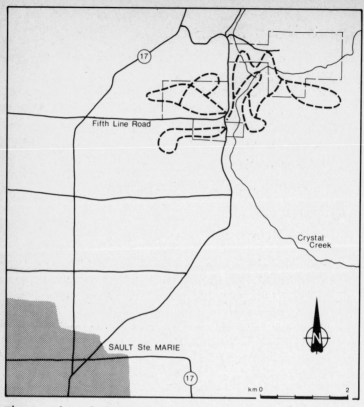

The Crystal Creek Trails (28)

purposes very well. A joint undertaking of the Sault Ste. Marie Conservation Authority, the Kinsmen Club, the Soo Finnish Ski Club, and the Ontario Ministry of Natural Resources, the trail loops in the Crystal Creek system radiate from a central lodge operated by the Soo Finnish Club.

The trails are well marked and offer some excellent north-country hiking and skiing.

Dundas Valley Trail System

Managing Organization:
   Hamilton Region Conservation Authority
   P. O. Box 7099
   838 Mineral Springs Road
   Ancaster, Ontario   L9G 3L3
   Telephone (416) 525-2181

Location: southern Ontario, Hamilton area

Length: 31 km total

Degree of Difficulty: easy

Comments: The Hamilton Region Conservation Authority has
assembled almost eight hundred fifty hectares of natural,
scenic, and historic properties in the Dundas valley west of the

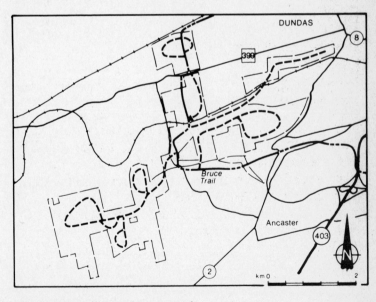

The Dundas Valley Trail System (29)

city of Hamilton. An excellent system of hiking, nature, and cross-country ski trails has been established throughout most of these lands.

Following a visit to the Trail Centre, a restored railway station located south of Highway #99 west of Dundas, visitors can choose from several trails that wind through the broad Dundas valley, which was formed by retreating glaciers some sixteen thousand years ago. This is a pleasant and varied landscape of woodland, rolling hills, and streams.

The Bruce Trail passes through the valley and shares several of the Conservation Authority's trail routes, thanks to a co-operative arrangement between the Hamilton Region Conservation Authority and the Bruce Trail Association.

Ganaraska Forest Trails

Managing Organization:
Ganaraska Region Conservation Authority
P. O. Box 328
Port Hope, Ontario   L1A 3W4
Telephone (416) 885-8173
Forest Centre (416) 797-2721

Location: south-central Ontario, Port Hope area.

Length: 110 km total

Degree of Difficulty: easy

Comments: The multi-purpose trail systems in this forty-two-hundred-hectare tract of land provide a good opportunity for some pleasant daytime outdoor exercise in an intensively managed forest reserve. No overnight camping is permitted.

Unlike the forests to be seen along the more northern Shield trails, the Ganaraska Forest is largely the result of many

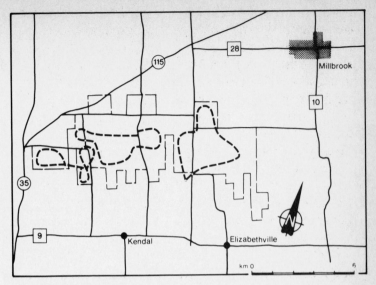

The Ganaraska Forest Trails (30)

years of reforestation on the rolling sandy soils left by retreating glaciers. Trails in the Ganaraska Forest range from hiking to cross-country skiing to snowmobiling and simple forest access roads. All of these can be used during summer months for pedestrian recreation.

Access to the Forest may be gained from Highway #28 north of Port Hope, or Highway #35/115 north of Newcastle.

K&P Trail

Managing Organization:
Mississippi Valley Conservation Authority
P. O. Box 268
Lanark, Ontario   KoG 1Ko
Telephone (613) 259-2421

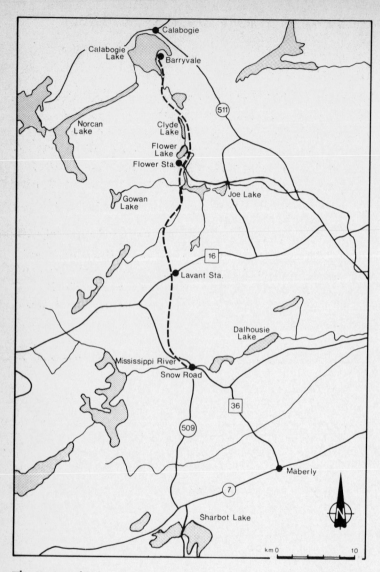

The K&P Trail (31)

Location: eastern Ontario. Snow Road north to Calabogie.

Length: 35 km

Degree of Difficulty: easy

Comments: The K&P Trail is a multi-purpose recreational trail which follows the old bed of the historic Kingston and Pembroke Railway. The railway was built between 1872 and 1884 and was abandoned after many years of profitable business hauling logs, sawn lumber, iron ore, and phosphate south to Kingston. Like the Seguin Trail in the Parry Sound District, this trail provides an excellent opportunity to experience the frontier history of the area.

While camping is not allowed on the trail, the Mississippi Valley Conservation Authority has excellent trail shelters and fireplaces. Hikers are advised to carry their own drinking water and are also asked to stay on the thirty-three-metre wide public trailway at all times as most of the route passes through private lands.

Laurentian Lake Trails

Managing Organization:
Nickel District Conservation Authority
West Tower, Civic Centre Square
20 Brady Street
Sudbury, Ontario   P3A 5K3
Telephone (705) 674-5249

Location: northern Ontario, Sudbury area

Length: 30 km total

Degree of Difficulty: easy

Comments: For many people the word "Sudbury" connotes an image of barren, rocky, almost lunar landscape devoid of vegetation or life of any kind. After almost a century of mining and smelting activity in the area this image is not too far from reality in some parts of the region. In recent years, however, co-operative efforts by government, industry, and Laurentian University have produced noticeable results in "greening" the area once again.

A visit to the interpretive and hiking trails of the Laurentian Lake Conservation Area is a good way to view examples of the area's plant and animal ecology and the complex geology of the southern edge of the Sudbury Basin.

The main trail follows the rock ridges, bogs, and beaver meadows around the irregular shoreline of Laurentian Lake. Shorter nature trails, ski and running trails, and abandoned bush roads also provide access to other parts of the more than one thousand hectares of this conservation area.

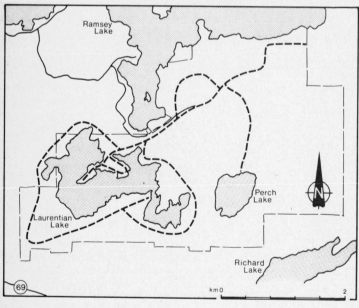

The Laurentian Lake Trails (32)

National Parks Trails

There are four national parks in Ontario; St. Lawrence Islands, Georgian Bay Islands, Point Pelee, and Pukaskwa. A new park has been proposed for the northern end of the Bruce Peninsula.

The following pages contain references to trails in three of the four existing national parks. St. Lawrence Islands National Park has not been listed due to its limited hiking trail facilities, although many of the islands in the park are worth exploring on foot.

Georgian Bay Islands National Park

Beausoleil Island Trails

Managing Organization:
Georgian Bay Islands National Park
P. O. Box 28
Honey Harbour, Ontario P0E 1E0
Telephone (705) 756-2415

Location: central Ontario, via Highway #501

Length: 30 km

Degree of Difficulty: easy to moderate

Comments: Although Beausoleil Island is small (only 1.6 km wide and 8 km long, or about 13.8 square km) it is one of the gems of Ontario's park trail system environments. It is but one of fifty islands in the park, and these are only a fraction of the famous thirty thousand islands scattered along the east side of Georgian Bay.

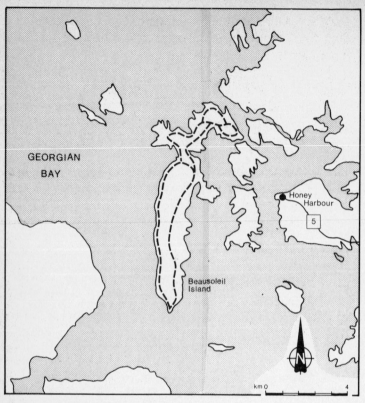

The Beausoleil Island Trails in Georgian Bay
Islands National Park (33)

Access to the island, subject to weather conditions, is
gained by way of private or rented boat or water taxi from
Honey Harbour.

There are 186 primitive campsites, available on a
first-come-first-served basis, located in eleven areas on the
island. These include some very scenic shore tent sites — some
of the best in Ontario, especially in the fall when the weather
and leaves are at their spectacular best.

The island has been divided into four zones, all linked by a
network of trails which, taken together, require some twenty
hours of hiking time. To get the most from any visit to the

island's smooth granite-and-pine character (the landscape captured on canvas by members of the Group of Seven), much more time should be taken.

Massasauga rattlesnakes (see page 114) are not uncommon on the island, so hikers should exercise some caution.

All in all, Beausoleil Island, along with other nearby public islands, are beautiful examples of Georgian Bay's eastern shoreline landscape; great to explore by boat and on foot.

Georgian Bay Islands National Park

Flowerpot Island Trails

Managing Organization:
Georgian Bay Islands National Park
P. O. Box 28
Honey Harbour, Ontario   PoE 1Eo
Telephone (705) 756-2415

Location: southern Ontario. 7 km off the tip of the Bruce Peninsula at Tobermory (access via Highway #6)

Length: 4 km (approximately)

Degree of Difficulty: easy to moderate

Comments: Hikers finishing their Bruce Trail hike in Tobermory may well want to complete their hiking holiday with a day-trip or overnight visit to Flowerpot Island. Although included in the Georgian Bay Islands National Park, Flowerpot Island is, geologically speaking, part of the Niagara Escarpment rather than the Pre-Cambrian granites and gneisses of the eastern Georgian Bay islands.

The distinctive "flowerpots," ten- to fifteen-metre high rock structures carved by centuries of pounding waves, wind, and ice, give this island its name. Seeing them is only one of

One of the distinctive "flowerpots" of Flowerpot Island in Georgian Bay Islands National Park.

the many reasons for making the trip from Tobermory by private or rented boat, or by the glass-bottomed tour boats, which stop frequently at this island. Many species of ferns, orchids, and other wildflowers are to be found along Flowerpot Island's three to four kilometres of trails.

Six campsites are available on a first-come-first-served basis upon arrangement with park staff, but no other facilities are available. Hikers should, therefore, be prepared to carry everything they will need for their visit, overnight or not.

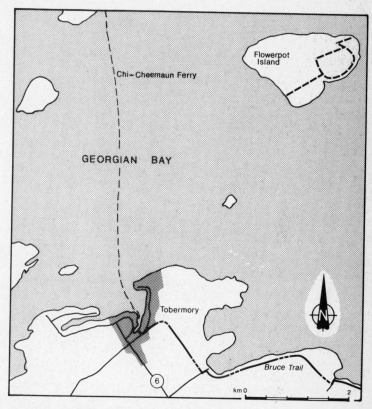

The Flowerpot Island Trails in Georgian Bay Islands National Park (34)

Point Pelee Trails

Managing Organization:
 Point Pelee National Park
 R. R. #1
 Leamington, Ontario   N8H 3V4
 Telephone
 (519) 326-3204 (Group Camping Reservations)
 (519) 326-1124 (Visitor Services Centre: General Information)

Location: southwestern Ontario. 56 km east of Windsor and Detroit on the north shore of Lake Erie (access via Highway #3).

Length: 10 to 12 km

Degree of Difficulty: easy. Some trails are suitable for handicapped persons.

Comments: The trails of Point Pelee are short nature interpretation trails rather than hiking trails, but because of the excellent opportunity they provide to view wildlife, they are a "must" for any hiker/naturalist.

 Point Pelee, a fifteen-kilometre peninsula jutting into Lake Erie, is the southernmost point of mainland Canada, and is renowned for its spectacular spring and fall congregations of migrating birds (with their accompanying multitudes of birdwatchers!). Because of its southern location, Point Pelee National Park also harbours species of plants (e.g., prickly pear cactus), reptiles (e.g., Blanding's turtle) and amphibians (e.g., Fowler's toad) not commonly found further north in Ontario, beyond the Carolinian, or Deciduous Forest Region.

 This is a popular park, rather crowded at times, and there are camping facilities only for organized groups upon

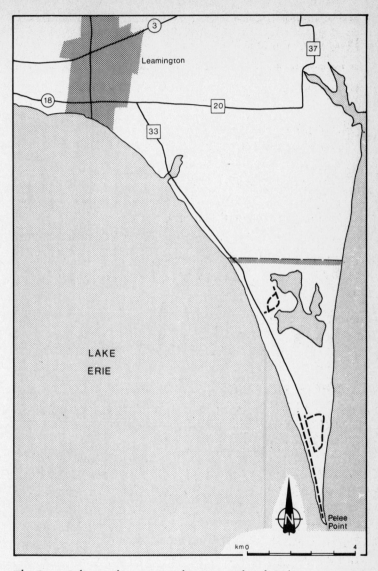

The Point Pelee Trails in Point Pelee National Park (35)

pre-registration. Additional camping is available nearby at Wheatley Provincial Park and at a number of commercial campgrounds.

All nature trails are well marked and maintained and include boardwalks extending several hundred metres into a large marsh that makes up almost fifty-seven per cent of the park's more than fourteen hundred hectares. Extraordinary views of several rare birds, reptiles, and amphibians are virtually guaranteed on all of Pelee's trails.

Pukaskwa National Park

Coastal Hiking Trail

Managing Organization:
    Pukaskwa National Park
    P. O. Box 550
    Marathon, Ontario   P0T 2E0
    Telephone (807) 229-0801

Location: northern Ontario. 400 km north of Sault Ste. Marie via Highways #17 and #627

Length: 70 km

Degree of Difficulty: very challenging

Comments: As suggested in the sections on the Voyageur Trail and Lake Superior Provincial Park, the shoreline of Lake Superior presents probably some of the best of wilderness hiking in Ontario. The combination of scenery, remoteness, and history (as well as pre-history) makes for a very rewarding hiking experience.

As Pukaskwa is a relatively new park, its trails, campsites, and other facilities are still being developed. Much has been done, however, and park staff have prepared several very useful brochures and booklets outlining the park's hiking, camping, and canoeing opportunities. There is no need for reservations in the park as yet, but all hikers should register, for safety reasons, at the trail head at Hattie Cove before starting out.

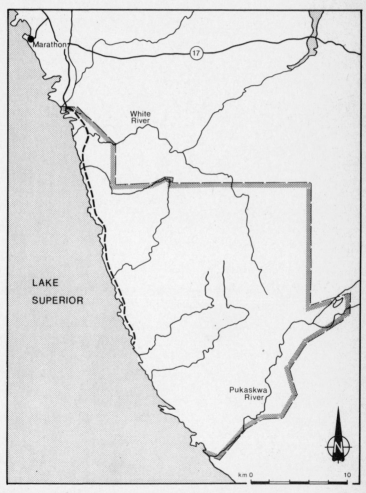

The Coastal Hiking Trail in Pukaskwa National Park (36)

Pukaskwa's beauty is, paradoxically, as delicate as it is austere. In using the park all visitors should do their utmost to leave no trace of their visit behind them. This extends beyond camping to walking as well. Hikers should, for example, strive to step only on bare rock or mineral soil, in order not to dislodge clumps of lichens or mosses which may have taken a century to colonize a footprint-sized site, and make every effort not to disturb any of the birds or animals encountered along the way.

The park contains a small herd of woodland caribou, at the southern edge of their range of distribution in Ontario, as well as many moose, wolf, black bear, lynx, and other interesting wildlife.

Other Trails

This final section describes a number of trails which, because they are not part of a province-wide management system, are not grouped in any of the previous four categories.

Generally, trails in this group are short — day-use or nature trails — and, while they may physically link up with some of the longer trails described earlier, they are managed by special-interest organizations which have a more local focus, perhaps, than that exercised by the Ontario Ministry of Natural Resources, Parks Canada, the Conservation Authorities, or the FOHTA organizations.

None of the trails in this section has camping facilities, as all are meant for day outings. As mentioned regarding many of the shorter trails described earlier, this should not prevent experienced hikers from using them to keep in trim or to hone their nature identification skills in preparation for longer trips.

These trails are located close to major urban centres and are thus ideal for "recharging" mental, spiritual, and emotional batteries after a hard day on the treadmill.

Kolapore Uplands Wilderness Ski Trails

Managing Organization:
   University of Toronto Outing Club
   P. O. Box 6647
   Postal Station "A"
   Toronto, Ontario   M5W 1X4

Location: southern Ontario, Collingwood–Meaford area.

Length: 49 km

Degree of Difficulty: easy to moderate

Comments: This system of thirteen cross-country ski trails managed by the University of Toronto Outing Club is located mainly on lands owned by the County of Grey, the Ontario Ministry of Natural Resources, and the North Grey Region Conservation Authority. Some parts of the trail also cross private land, so trail users must follow the Trail User's Code at all times. Although designed as cross-country ski trails, the Kolapore Uplands trails also provide pleasant hiking opportunities in spring, summer and fall.

The system is marked with triangular orange blazes. Neither camping nor fires are permitted.

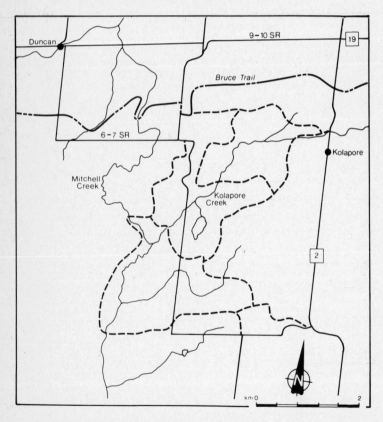

The Kolapore Uplands Wilderness Ski Trails (37)

Merrittrail

Managing Organization:
   Welland Canals Preservation Association
   P. O. Box 1224
   52 Lakeport Road
   St. Catharines, Ontario   L2R 7A7
   Telephone (416) 934-6884

Location: southern Ontario, St. Catharines area

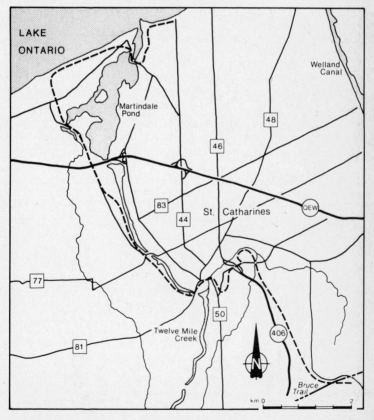

The Merrittrail (38)

Length: 33 km

Degree of Difficulty: easy

Comments: The Merrittrail is an urban bicycle/walking trail which winds along the route of three of the earlier Welland Canals built during the 1800s. The trail starts at the Mountain Locks on the Niagara Escarpment and follows streets and pathways north through St. Catharines to Port Dalhousie on Lake Ontario.

In spite of its urban character — or perhaps because of it — this is an excellent trail for exploring the history of the area. The hiker will not only learn about the building of the canals, but also about the settlement of the area and its role in the War of 1812, while enjoying as well the geology, flora, and fauna of the Niagara Peninsula.

Niagara Glen Nature Area Trails

Managing Organization:
Niagara Parks Commission
P. O. Box 150
Department "B"
Niagara Falls, Ontario   L2E 6T2
Telephone (416) 356-2241

Location: southern Ontario, Niagara Falls area.

Length: 4 km

Degree of Difficulty: easy

Comments: To most people the words *Niagara Falls* evoke the Falls themselves and their surrounding tourist-oriented development. Since the late 1800s, however, the Niagara Parks Commission has been managing large tracts of historic and scenic natural land along the Niagara Gorge downstream from

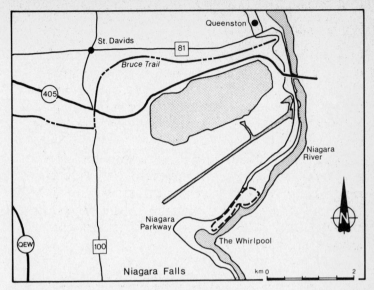

The Niagara Glen Nature Area Trails (39)

the Falls to Niagara-on-the-Lake. A number of short but very interesting nature trails which allow visitors to explore the Carolinian flora and geology of the Gorge have been established.

Access to these trails is free and parking is available at well-marked parking areas along the Niagara Parkway. No camping is allowed along the Niagara Parks System trails, but several commercial campgrounds — which also serve Bruce Trail hikers — are located in the area.

Many nature interpretation trails are set up so as to allow a close approach to wildlife while disturbing it as little as possible.

Royal Botanical Gardens Nature Trails

Managing Organization:
  Royal Botanical Gardens
  P. O. Box 399
  Hamilton, Ontario   L8N 3H8
  Telephone (416) 527-1158

Location: southern Ontario, Hamilton area

Length: 34 km total

Degree of Difficulty: easy

Comments: The Royal Botanical Gardens is a complex of natural lands and intensively managed gardens of horticultural interest in the Hamilton–Dundas–Burlington area at the west end of Lake Ontario. Many trails have been developed to allow visitors to explore the fascinating natural history of "Cootes Paradise" (a marshy bay west of Hamilton Harbour and a

Southern Ontario's hundreds of kilometres of nature trails attract birdwatchers and other nature lovers.

favourite resting area for many species of waterfowl uncommon to the area), the Niagara Escarpment, and the Grindstone Creek (or Hendrie) Valley.

Detailed maps and an impressive selection of scientific research papers prepared by Royal Botanical Gardens staff are available at the RBG headquarters, located at 680 Plains Road West (old Highway #2) in Burlington.

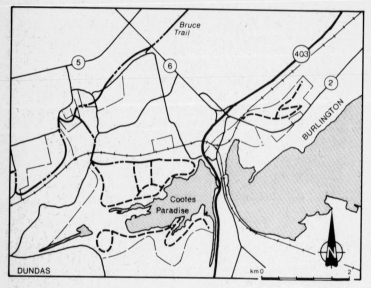

The Royal Botanical Gardens Nature Trails (40)

An aerial view of part of Cootes Paradise with McMaster University in the background.

In more northern parts of Ontario, the black bear is a common sight. Black bears can weigh up to 300 kg and are omnivorous. "Live and let live" is a good maxim for the hiker to follow where this trail user is concerned.

Health & Safety Tips

Although Ontario's trails should present few problems for hikers who have properly readied themselves and their equipment and have planned their trip well, a number of dangers may arise that could turn a fun hike into an uncomfortable experience — even into a tragedy. The many excellent references listed in "Other Reading" deal with these hazards in greater detail, but a number of them are worth pointing out here. Hikers are advised to be aware of them, anticipate them, and, preferably, know how to avoid them.

Hypothermia

Hypothermia can be a silent killer if the hiker is not alert to the combination of factors that bring it about.

Literally, the word means "below (i.e., below normal) heat," and refers to the dangerous lowering of the body's core temperature. At around 37°C the body functions well. It is capable of carrying on normally provided the supply of fuel is not outstripped by the body's metabolic processes. Under ideal weather conditions, a hiker with a generally good state of health can expect to maintain a good balance between the body heat produced and the heat lost. Under adverse weather conditions, however, long hard exercise can combine with a low input of energy food and cold wet clothing to seriously upset this balance. A slow but steady drain of heat out of the body begins. Surprisingly, this may happen more quickly in temperatures above 0°C than in sub-zero temperatures, especially if insulation is inadequate or becomes water-soaked in a cold drizzle or wind-driven rain.

The best defence against hypothermia is to avoid it. Before the season starts, the hiker should get into good physical shape. All trips should be planned meticulously, mapping each day's travelling so as not to overextend the body's capabilities. Distances always turn out to be longer, and the terrain rougher, than they appear on the map. On the trail, the hiker should take in plenty of substantial, high-energy food and hot drinks to maintain the body's core temperature. Clothing should be adequate for the season's extremes and rain gear should be a part of every pack. Several thin layers of clothing are better than one or two thick ones; items can be added or removed depending on the level of activity and external conditions. Above all, the body's signals should be monitored at all times; one of the dangers of hypothermia is the failure of the victim to recognize in the early stages that the process has started.

At first, the hiker may simply feel cold after sweating during heavy activity, and sense a need to get warmed up. If this early symptom is ignored, shivering may begin, accompanied by numbness in the extremities. Before long, the shivering becomes almost uncontrollable, even violent. Co-ordination may be lost, the hiker may stumble (a danger in itself in rough terrain), and speech may become incoherent. The victim may become irrational and slip in and out of consciousness, the periods of unconsciousness becoming longer until the vital bodily functions — brain, heart, lungs — simply stop. All for want of some common sense and foresight.

The treatment for hypothermia is relatively simple, but quick action may be crucial for the victim's survival: the body's core temperature must be returned to normal as soon as possible. Heat must be added to the inside of the body (by drinking hot liquids, even hot water) and to the outside (via direct radiant heat from a fire, other warm bodies, or a warm bath, if available). Simply piling on clothing or blankets may actually hinder the warming-up process by preventing vital external heat from reaching the body. Medical help should be sought as soon as possible.

Hypothermia may be encountered anywhere, on any trail, even on a short day hike, but conditions in the spring and fall may make a hiker more susceptible to it.

Plants

While there are many delicious wild nuts, berries, and roots free for the taking along Ontario's trails (see the list of references in "Other Reading"), there are also many that are poisonous or that may be otherwise damaging to the health and comfort of the hiker.

Three shiny green leaves drooping away from a central stem are a clue to this plant's identity. Poison ivy; do not touch!

Unless you are familiar with plants you think will make a nice snack, don't eat them!

In the realm of non-edible plants, poison ivy comes immediately to mind. Physical contact with its shiny green leaves or its stems can break open plant cells, releasing a volatile oil that greatly irritates the skin and causes severe itching and open blisters. The fluid from these can spread the rash to other parts of the body or to other people. Even inhaling smoke from burning poison ivy plants can produce severe damage to the respiratory tract, so campfires should be carefully located and controlled. Since poison ivy is a common plant in southern Ontario, hikers should learn to recognize it in its single plant form, vine form, and as a colony.

Animals

Although no animals present a general threat to the safety of hikers in Ontario some species can, under certain circumstances, be dangerous.

Black bears are relatively common in northern and central Ontario and are often a nuisance to campers and cottagers who fail to keep food or garbage out of their reach. In some areas, scavenger bears accustomed to humans have come to equate them with free meals; considerable danger may exist when these animals lose their natural wariness and boldly wander into campsites. Any bear encountered along Ontario's trails is a wild animal and should be respectfully avoided — especially if there are cubs in the vicinity. In camp, all food and unburned waste (which should be packed out at the end of the hike) must be strung up in a tree a hundred metres or more from the tent site, at least three metres above the ground, and two metres from any branches or the tree trunk. Never should food of any kind be kept in the tent; this is an open invitation for any keen-nosed bear who may visit the campsite, and the consequences are obvious.

The sonorous, echoing, night-time howl of the timber wolf is a sound never to be forgotten, but hikers will have to be very lucky to catch a glimpse of this shy animal.

The Massasauga rattlesnake, a mottled brown rattler and Ontario's only venomous snake, is relatively common in the upper Bruce Peninsula (along the Bruce Trail), along the eastern shore of Georgian Bay (Killbear Provincial Park), and on many islands in Georgian Bay Islands National Park (e.g., Flowerpot Island and Beausoleil Island).

Usually unaggressive and less than ninety centimetres in length, a rattler will normally retreat when it senses ground vibrations from approaching footsteps. Once warned, it will usually (but not always) sound a dry buzz, similar to that of a cicada, by quickly vibrating rattles at the end of its tail. A hiker who hears this sound should immediately stop, look carefully around, and proceed slowly, giving the snake a wide berth. The snake, after all, has as much right to the trail as has the hiker. A hiker about to sit down for a rest or to reach up for a hand hold on a rocky ledge may get a nasty bite without any warning. Such unpleasantness can be avoided easily just by checking ahead first.

Although the Massasauga rattler's venom is very toxic, the

Although its bite is venomous, hikers actually have little reason to fear the Massasauga rattler, a snake that would invariably rather run than fight.

amount inflicted is usually small, due to the snake's short striking range and relatively short fangs. The heavy clothing usually worn by hikers also diminishes the effect of snakebite. Nevertheless, there may still be enough venom to make the victim seriously ill, so emergency medical help should be sought immediately. All major hospitals around Georgian Bay have antivenin vaccine on hand. These centres are listed in the *Bruce Trail Guidebook* and in published material about other trails in the Massasauga's area.

Emergency treatment can be given on the trail until proper medical help is obtained. Since the venom contains enzymes that attack and break down blood cells, the victim should be kept as still as possible. This will reduce the spread of venom through the body via the blood stream and lymphatic system. A tourniquet — properly located and applied — may be used. A snakebite kit, consisting of a small suction device, a sterilized razor blade for incising puncture wounds, antiseptic, and bandage may be a useful addition to the pack first aid kit. Such kits are available at some drug stores and most sporting goods stores. Any kit will be of little benefit if improperly used, however, so hikers should thoroughly familiarize themselves with their kit instructions as part of their pre-trip planning.

Rabies, which attacks the nervous system, has rarely resulted in a human fatality in Ontario, thanks to the improved availability of anti-rabies vaccine. Deaths from rabies among wild and domestic animals, however, are common. Southern Ontario has the highest incidence of rabies in North America. The disease tends to be cyclical, with outbreaks in different parts of the province over a period of several years. Foxes and skunks are the primary vectors of rabies in Ontario, although bats, coyotes, raccoons, and other very mobile animals can be infected. Domestic farm animals and pet dogs and cats are also common carriers. The disease virus is transmitted to humans through bites, scratches, or simply from the infected animal's saliva coming into contact with open wounds or the mucous membranes in the eyes, nose, and mouth.

Rabid animals in advanced stages of the disease usually show abnormal behaviour. They exhibit an apparent lack of fear toward humans, erratic movements, and excessive salivation.

Hikers should avoid contact with any wild or domestic animal that appears to behave strangely. All pets accompanying hikers should be kept on a leash. If a hiker is bitten — or even if it is suspected that an animal that was touched has rabies — the wound or the affected part should be washed thoroughly with soap and water, antiseptic applied, and then the victim should get to a hospital as soon as possible for treatment. The incident should be immediately reported to the nearest Ontario or federal agricultural department office, police station, veterinarian, or conservation officer.

Mosquitos & Blackflies

Mosquitos and blackflies can be almost intolerably annoying from mid-May to late August in most parts of the province. In both cases, it is the females of the species, requiring a meal of blood to produce eggs, which descend by the thousands on undeserving hikers. These pests can turn an otherwise uneventful hike into a memorable experience.

There are several things a hiker can do to reduce the aggravation of the buzzing hordes and the itchy bites.

If a camping area is large enough, placing and orienting the tent to make the best use of any breezes would be a good start (e.g., on a point of land, on a lakeshore or on a hill). In addition, perfumes, aftershave lotions, and other such artificial scents that may act as an "odour beacon" for an insect testing the air for signs of a meal should not be worn.

Wearing light-coloured clothing will also reduce the attractiveness of the human blood-bank. Research indicates that both mosquitos and blackflies seem to favour people wearing dark clothing. Cuffs that fit tightly at the ankles and wrists will also reduce the number of bites considerably.

Finally, hikers should also carry a supply of a good insect repellent. Lotions are messier than spray cans but are easier to carry. Any repellent containing a high percentage of N.N-Diethyl-M-Toluamide (e.g., 95% or so) will do the job.

Getting Lost

This subject may seem a trifle out of place in a discussion of hazards to the hiker following well-marked trails. On some of Ontario's more remote trail systems, however, where roads and fences are non-existent and marking may not be quite up to par, even the most experienced hiker may miss a turn in the trail or become disoriented during a brief sortie away from camp.

As with most other hazards, the problem is best avoided by proper advance planning at the outset. Careful study of trail and topographic maps (a chronic activity of some dyed-in-the-wool hikers during long winter evenings at home) can produce a certain basic familiarity with the trail and its environs. A hiker thus primed will usually have a better idea of what to expect and will be less prone to becoming "temporarily disoriented." Trail-marking systems, which differ from trail to trail, should be studied as well, as should the descriptive text that usually accompanies most trail maps.

Maps and compass should always be kept close at hand during hikes for frequent reference. Even on short outings the ever-present day-pack should contain these two important items amongst its other emergency supplies.

A hiker who suddenly realizes that the trail has somehow disappeared can usually find the route quite easily by retracing steps to the last visible blaze, studying the guide map, and locating the next marker in the proper direction.

Getting thoroughly lost in the bush is much more serious. More exacting orientation and effort may be required to regain the trail. Above all, the hiker should not panic and simply walk in what seems to be the right direction. This inevitably turns out to be a circle or a figure eight and will only result in exhaustion and wasted time. The first step is to stop, then sit down, look around, study the map, read the compass, and carefully plot a return course.

If night falls on a lost hiker, an emergency camp should be made on the spot. Travel in the bush at night can be dangerous; the problem may be seriously compounded by a sprained ankle or worse.

On trails in the more settled areas of southern Ontario, becoming lost is less likely and somewhat less dangerous. Most trails cross travelled roads or pass near human settlement of some form where help may be obtained.

A warning here, however. Hikers should not bother residents near a trail, except in an emergency. Many a section of trail crossing private land has been closed because hikers overstepped the bounds of hospitality extended by landowners once too often, waking residents late at night to ask for directions, use a telephone, ask for water, etc. For anyone leading a hike, scouting the entire route before the scheduled hike is a "must," for legal reasons as well as for the comfort and safety of hikers.

Hunting

Throughout the province at certain times of the year (usually in October and November), the Ontario Ministry of Natural Resources may designate hunting seasons on bear, deer, moose, and small game birds and animals. The areas open to hunting and the length of the season vary widely from region to region and from year to year, depending on the ministry's assessment of animal populations.

Hiking on some trails during these periods may be somewhat hazardous if certain precautions are not taken. First, hikers should inquire at the appropriate district office of the Ministry of Natural Resources about local hunting restrictions. Second, hikers should try to be as conspicuous as possible. They should wear their brightest clothing and stay clear of known hunting areas. Hanging a few metal pots on the outside of the pack, or making some other kind of noise will lessen the risk as well.

The chances of a hunting mishap involving a hiker are very low, but the large numbers of hunters in some areas (e.g., areas of "controlled hunts" in parts of southern Ontario) could conceivably result in injury to the unwary trail user.

The moose, the largest member of the deer family, may weigh more than 550 kg.
Hikers on central and northern trails might encounter moose.

Water Quality

On most of the remote northern hiking trails, water found in
clear, cool, fast-running streams or open lakes may be used
without treatment. In southern Ontario, farming activity and
urban development have made most surface water
undrinkable without treatment with Halazone, chlorine, or by
thorough boiling.

   Trail guides will usually indicate sources of potable water.
Whatever the trail, instructions in the guides or posted on the
site should be followed. Whenever there is any doubt, water
should be well boiled or not used at all.

Forest Fires

Every year in Ontario, forest fires destroy thousands of hectares of bush, kill countless birds and animals, and often threaten human life and property. Many such fires are started by people — campers, hunters, fishermen, perhaps even hikers — smoking carelessly or failing to extinguish campfires.

Every hiker should do everything possible to prevent forest fires. A small stove is preferable to a campfire for cooking. If a campfire is used, it should be located properly and the fire should be kept small and under control. Naturally, it should be thoroughly extinguished when camp is broken; doused repeatedly with water and the ashes stirred until the fire is dead out.

The Ontario Ministry of Natural Resources publicises a forest fire index during fire season. This index may change from day to day depending on weather conditions. At all times hikers should know and abide by the fire regulations in effect in the area of their hike. (See Appendix 2 for the MNR district office closest to the trail being used.)

Appendix 1

The following reprinting of the *Occupier's Liability Act* and the *Trespass to Property Act* is provided for information only. For legal purposes, reference should be made to the original statutes.

An informative booklet entitled *Property Protection and Outdoor Opportunities* is available free from the Ontario Ministry of the Attorney General, Communications Branch, 18 King Street East, 18th Floor, Toronto, Ontario, M5C 1C5.

An Act Respecting Occupier's Liability

Her Majesty, by and with the advice and consent of the Legislative Assembly of the Province of Ontario, enacts as follows:

1. In this Act,
    a) "occupier" includes,
        i)   a person who is in physical possession of premises, or
        ii) a person who has responsibility for and control over the condition of premises or the activities there carried on, or control over persons allowed to enter the premises, notwithstanding that there is more than one occupier of the same premises;
    b) "premises" means lands and structures, or either of them, and includes,
        i)   water,
        ii) ships and vessels,
        iii) trailers and portable structures designed or used for residence, business or shelter,
        iv) trains, railway cars, vehicles and aircraft, except while in operation.

2. Subject to section 9, the provisions of this Act apply in place of the rules of the common law that determine the care that the occupier of premises at common law is required to show for the purpose of determining his liability in law in respect of

dangers to persons entering on the premises or the property brought on the premises by those persons.

3. 1) An occupier of premises owes a duty to take such care as in all the circumstances of the case is reasonable to see that persons entering on the premises, and the property brought on the premises by those persons are reasonably safe while on the premises.

   2) The duty of care provided for in subsection 1 applies whether the danger is caused by the condition of the premises or by an activity carried on on the premises.

   3) The duty of care provided for in subsection 1 applies except in so far as the occupier of premises is free to and does restrict, modify or exclude his duty.

4. 1) The duty of care provided for in subsection 1 of section 3 does not apply in respect of risks willingly assumed by the person who enters on the premises but in that case the occupier owes a duty to the person to not create a danger with the deliberate intent of doing harm or damage to the person or his property and to not act with reckless disregard of the presence of the person or his property.

   2) A person who is on premises with the intention of committing, or in the commission of, a criminal act shall be deemed to have willingly assumed all risks and is subject to the duty of care set out in subsection 1.

   3) A person who enters premises described in subsection 4 shall be deemed to have willingly assumed all risks and is subject to the duty of care set out in subsection 1,

      a) where the entry is prohibited under *The Trespass to Property Act, 1980;*

      b) where the occupier has posted no notice in respect of entry and has not otherwise expressly permitted entry; or

      c) where the entry is for the purpose of a recreational activity and,

         i) no fee is paid for the entry or activity of the person, other than a benefit or payment received from a government or government agency or a non-profit recreation club or association, and

ii) the person is not being provided with living accommodation by the occupier.

4) The premises referred to in subsection 3 are,
   a) a rural premises that is,
      i) used for agricultural purposes, including land under cultivation, orchards, pastures, woodlots and farm ponds,
      ii) vacant or undeveloped premises,
      iii) forested or wilderness premises;
   b) golf courses when not open for playing;
   c) utility rights-of-way and corridors, excluding structures located thereon;
   d) unopened road allowances;
   e) private roads reasonably marked by notice as such; and
   f) recreational trails reasonably marked by notice as such.

5. 1) The duty of an occupier under this Act, or his liability for breach thereof, shall not be restricted or excluded by the provisions of any contract to which the person to whom the duty is owed is not a party, whether or not the occupier is bound by the contract to permit such person to enter or use the premises.

   2) A contract shall not by virtue of this Act have the effect, unless it expressly so provides, of making an occupier who has taken reasonable care, liable to any person not a party to the contract, for dangers due to the faulty execution of any work of construction, maintenance or repair, or other like operation by persons other than himself, his servants, and persons acting under his direction and control.

   3) Where an occupier is free to restrict, modify or exclude his duty of care or his liability for breach thereof, he shall take reasonable steps to bring such restriction, modification or exclusion to the attention of the person to whom the duty is owed.

6. 1) Where damage to any person or his property is caused by the negligence of an independent contractor employed by the occupier, the occupier is not on that account liable if in all the circumstances he had acted reasonably in entrusting the work to the independent contractor, if he had taken

such steps, if any, as he reasonably ought in order to satisfy himself that the contractor was competent and that the work had been properly done, and if it was reasonable that the work performed by the independent contractor should have been undertaken.

2) Where there is more than one occupier of premises, any benefit accruing by reason of subsection 1 to the occupier who employed the independent contractor shall accrue to all occupiers of the premises.

3) Nothing in this section affects any duty of the occupier that is non-delegable at common law or affects any provision in any other Act that provides that an occupier is liable for the negligence of an independent contractor.

7. In so far as subsections 1 and 2 of section 5 prevent the duty of care owed by an occupier, or liability for breach thereof, from being restricted or excluded, they apply to contracts entered into both before and after the commencement of this Act, and in so far as section 6 enlarges the duty of care owed by an occupier, or liability for breach thereof, it applies only in respect of contracts entered into after the commencement of this Act.

8. 1) Where premises are occupied or used by virtue of a tenancy under which the landlord is responsible for the maintenance or repair of the premises, it is the duty of the landlord to show towards any person or the property brought on the premises by those persons, the same duty of care in respect of dangers arising from any failure on his part in carrying out his responsibility as is required by this Act to be shown by an occupier of the premises.

2) For the purposes of this section, a landlord shall not be deemed to have made default in carrying out any obligation to a person unless his default is such as to be actionable at the suit of the person entitled to possession of the premises.

3) For the purposes of this section, obligations imposed by any enactment by virtue of a tenancy shall be treated as imposed by the tenancy and "tenancy" includes a statutory tenancy, an implied tenancy and any contract conferring the right of occupation, and "landlord" shall be construed accordingly.

4) This section applies to all tenancies whether created before or after the commencement of this Act.

9. 1) Nothing in this Act relieves an occupier of premises in any particular case from any higher liability or any duty to show a higher standard of care that in that case is incumbent on him by virtue of any enactment or rule of law imposing special liability or standards of care on particular classes of persons including, but without restricting the generality of the foregoing, the obligations of,

    a) innkeepers, subject to *The Innkeepers Act;*
    b) common carriers;
    c) bailees.

2) Nothing in this Act shall be construed to affect the rights, duties and liabilities resulting from a master and servant relationship where it exists.

3) the provisions of *The Negligence Act* apply with respect to causes of action to which this Act applies.

10. 1) This Act binds the Crown, subject to *The Proceedings Against the Crown Act.*

2) This Act does not apply to the Crown or to any municipal corporation, where the Crown or the municipal corporation is an occupier of a public highway or a public road.

11. This Act does not affect rights and liabilities of persons in respect of causes of action arising before this Act comes into force.

12. This Act comes into force on a day to be named by proclamation of the Lieutenant Governor.

13. The short title of this Act is *The Occupier's Liability Act, 1980.*

An Act to Protect Against Trespass to Property

Her Majesty, by and with the advice and consent of the Legislative Assembly of the Province of Ontario, enacts as follows:

1. 1) In this Act,
    a) "occupier" includes,
       i) a person who is in physical possession of premises, or
       ii) a person who has responsibility for and control over the condition of premises or the activities there carried on, or control over persons allowed to enter the premises, notwithstanding that there is more than one occupier of the same premises.
    b) "premises" means lands and structures, or either of them, and includes,
       i)   water,
       ii) ships and vessels,
       iii) trailers and portable structures designed or used for residence, business or shelter,
       iv) trains, railway cars, vehicles and aircraft, except while in operation.
    2) A school board has all the rights and duties of an occupier in respect of its school sites as defined in *The Education Act, 1974*.

2. 1) every person who is not acting under a right or authority conferred by law and who,
    a) without the express permission of the occupier, the proof of which rests on the defendant,
       i) enters on premises when entry is prohibited under this Act, or
       ii) engages in an activity on premises when the activity is prohibited under this Act; or
    b) does not leave the premises immediately after he is directed to do so by the occupier of the premises or a person authorized by the occupier,
    is guilty of an offence and on conviction is liable to a fine of not more than $1,000.
    2) It is a defence to a charge under subsection 1 in respect of premises that is land that the person charged reasonably

believed that he had title to or an interest in the land that entitled him to do the act complained of.

3. 1) Entry on premises may be prohibited by notice to that effect and entry is prohibited without any notice on premises,
   a) that is a garden, field or other land that is under cultivation, including a lawn, orchard, vineyard and premises on which trees have been planted and have not attained an average height of more than two metres and woodlots on land used primarily for agricultural purposes, or
   b) that is enclosed in a manner that indicates the occupier's intention to keep persons off the premises or to keep animals on the premises.

   2) There is presumption that access for lawful purposes to the door of a building on premises by a means apparently provided and used for the purpose of access is not prohibited.

4. 1) Where notice is given that one or more particular activities are permitted, all other activities and entry for the purpose are prohibited and any additional notice that entry is prohibited or a particular activity is prohibited on the same premises shall be construed to be for greater certainty only.

   2) Where entry on premises is not prohibited under section 3 or by notice that one or more particular activities are permitted under subsection 1, and notice is given that a particular activity is prohibited, that activity and entry for the purpose is prohibited and all other activities and entry for the purpose are not prohibited.

5. 1) A notice under this Act may be given,
   a) orally or in writing,
   b) by means of signs posted so that a sign is clearly visible in daylight under normal conditions from the approach to each ordinary point of access to the premises to which it applies; or
   c) by means of the marking system set out in section 7.

2) Substantial compliance with clause *b* or *c* of subsection 1 is sufficient notice.

6. 1) A sign naming an activity or showing a graphic representation of an activity is sufficient for the purposes of giving notice that the activity is permitted.

2) A sign naming an activity with an oblique line drawn through the name or showing a graphic representation of an activity with an oblique line drawn through the representation is sufficient for the purposes of giving notice that the activity is prohibited.

7. 1) Red markings made and posted in accordance with subsections 3 and 4 are sufficient for the purpose of giving notice that entry on the premises is prohibited.

2) Yellow markings made and posted in accordance with subsections 3 and 4 are sufficient for the purpose of giving notice that entry is prohibited except for the purpose of certain activities and shall be deemed to be notice of the activities permitted.

3) A marking under this section shall be of such a size that a circle ten centimeters in diameter can be contained wholly within it.

4) Markings under this section shall be so placed that a marking is clearly visible in daylight under normal conditions from the approach to each ordinary point of access to the premises to which it applies.

8. A notice or permission under this Act may be given in respect of any part of the premises of an occupier.

9. 1) A police officer, or the occupier of premises, or a person authorized by the occupier may arrest without warrant any person he believes on reasonable and probable grounds to be on the premises in contravention of section 2.

2) where the person who makes an arrest under subsection 1 is not a police officer, he shall promptly call for the assistance of a police officer and give the person arrested into the custody of the police officer.

3) A police officer to whom the custody of a person is given under subsection 2 shall be deemed to have arrested the

person for the purposes of the provision of *The Provincial Offences Act, 1979* applying to his release or continued detention and bail.

10. Where a police officer believes on reasonable and probable grounds that a person has been in contravention of section 2 and has made fresh departure from the premises, and the person refuses to give his name and address, or there are reasonable and probable grounds to believe that the name or address given is false, the police officer may arrest the person without warrant.

11. Where an offence under this Act is committed by means of a motor vehicle, as defined in the *The Highway Traffic Act*, the driver of the motor vehicle is liable to a fine provided under this Act and, where the driver is not the owner, the owner of the motor vehicle is liable to the fine provided under this Act unless the driver is convicted of the offence or, at the time the offence was committed, the motor vehicle was in the possession of a person other than the owner without the owner's consent.

12. 1) Where a person is convicted of an offence under section 2, and a person has suffered damage caused by the person convicted during the commission of the offence, the court shall, on the request of the prosecutor and with the consent of the person who suffered the damage, determine the damages and shall make a judgement for damages against the person convicted in favour of the person who suffered the damage, but no judgement shall be for an amount in excess of $1,000.

    2) Where a prosecution under section 2 is conducted by a private prosecutor, and the defendant is convicted, unless the court is of the opinion that the prosecution was not necessary for the protection of the occupier or his interests, the court shall determine the actual costs reasonably incurred in conducting the prosecution and, notwithstanding section 61 of *The Provincial Offences Act, 1979*, shall order those costs to be paid by the defendant to the prosecutor.

3) A judgement for damages under subsection 1, or an award of costs under subsection 2, shall be in addition to any fine that is imposed under the Act.

4) A judgement for damages under subsection 1 extinguishes the right of the person in whose favour the judgement is made to bring a civil action for damages against the person convicted arising out of the same facts.

5) The failure to request or refusal to grant a judgement for damages under subsection 1 does not affect a right to bring a civil action for damages arising out of the same facts.

6) The judgement for damages under subsection 1, and the award for costs under subsection 2, may be filed in a small claims court and shall be deemed to be a judgement or order of that court for the purposes of enforcement.

13. *The Petty Trespass Act*, being chapter 347 of the Revised Statutes of Ontario, 1970, is repealed.

14. The Act comes into force on a day to be named by proclamation of the Lieutenant Governor.

15. The short title of this Act is *The Trespass to Property Act, 1980*.

Appendix 2

Ministry of Natural Resources District Offices

Algonquin Park District
P. O. Box 219
Whitney, Ontario   K0J 2M0
(705) 633-5572

Atikokan District
108 Saturn Avenue
Atikokan, Ontario   P0T 1C0
(807) 597-6971

Aylmer District
353 Talbot Street West
Aylmer, Ontario   N5H 2S8
(519) 773-9241

Bancroft District
P. O. Box 500
Bancroft, Ontario   K0L 1C0
(613) 332-3940

Blind River District
62 Queen Street
P. O. Box 190
Blind River, Ontario   P0R 1B0
(705) 356-2234

Bracebridge District
P. O. Box 1138
Bracebridge, Ontario   P0B 1C0
(705) 645-8747

Brockville District
101 Water Street West
Brockville, Ontario   K6V 5Y8
(613) 342-8524

Cambridge District
P. O. Box 2186
Cambridge, Ontario   N3C 2W1
(519) 658-9355

Carleton Place District
10 Findlay Avenue
Carleton Place, Ontario   K7C 3Z6
(613) 257-5735

Chapleau District
34 Birch Street,
Chapleau, Ontario   P0M 1K0
(705) 864-1710

Chatham District
Kent County Municipal Building
435 Grand Avenue West
P. O. Box 1168
Chatham, Ontario   N7M 5L8
(519) 354-7340

Cochrane District
2 Third Avenue
P. O. Box 730
Cochrane, Ontario   P0L 1C0
(705) 272-4365

Cornwall District
113 Amelia Street
P. O. Box 1749
Cornwall, Ontario   K6H 5V7
(613) 933-1774

Dryden District
P. O. Box 730
Dryden, Ontario   P8N 2Z4
(807) 223-3341

Espanola District
P. O. Box 1340
Espanola, Ontario   P0P 1C0
(705) 869-1330

Fort Frances District
922 Scott Street
Fort Frances, Ontario   P9A 1J4
(807) 274-5337

Geraldton District
P. O. Box 640
Geraldton, Ontario   P0T 1M0
(807) 854-1030

Gogama District
P. O. Box 129
Gogama, Ontario   P0M 1W0
(705) 894-2000

Hearst District
P. O. Box 670
Hearst, Ontario   P0L 1N0
(705) 362-4346

Huronia District
Midhurst, Ontario   L0L 1X0
(705) 728-2900

Ignace District
P. O. Box 448
Ignace, Ontario   P0T 1T0
(807) 934-2233

Kapuskasing District
6 Government Road
Kapuskasing, Ontario   P5N 2W4
(705) 335-6191

Kenora District
P. O. Box 5080
808 Robertson Street
Kenora, Ontario   P9N 3X9
(807) 468-9841

Kirkland Lake District
P. O. Box 129
Swastika, Ontario   P0K 1T0
(705) 642-3222

Lindsay District
Ontario Government Building
322 Kent Street West
Lindsay, Ontario   K9V 4T7
(705) 324-6121

Maple District
Maple, Ontario   L0J 1E0
(416) 832-2761

Minden District
Minden, Ontario   K0M 2K0
(705) 286-1521

Moosonee District
P. O. Box 190
Moosonee, Ontario   P0L 1Y0
(705) 336-2987

Napanee District
1 Richmond Blvd.
Napanee, Ontario   K7R 3S3
(613) 354-2173

Niagara District
P. O. Box 1070
Fonthill, Ontario   L0S 1E0
(416) 892-2656

Nipigon District
P. O. Box 970
Nipigon, Ontario   P0T 2J0
(807) 887-2120

North Bay District
P. O. Box 3070
North Bay, Ontario   P1B 8K7
(705) 474-5550

Owen Sound District
611-9th Avenue East
Owen Sound, Ontario   N4K 3E4
(519) 376-3860

Parry Sound District
4 Miller Street
Parry Sound, Ontario   P2A 1S8
(705) 746-4201

Pembroke District
Riverside Drive
P. O. Box 220
Pembroke, Ontario   K8A 6X4
(613) 732-3661

Red Lake District
P. O. Box 323
Red Lake, Ontario   P0V 2M0
(807) 727-2531

Sault Ste. Marie District
P. O. Box 130
69 Church Street
Sault Ste. Marie, Ontario
P6A 5L5
(705) 949-1231

Simcoe District
645 Norfolk Street North
Simcoe, Ontario   N3Y 3R2
(519) 426-7650

Sioux Lookout District
P. O. Box 309
Sioux Lookout, Ontario   P0V 2T0
(807) 737-1140

Sudbury District
P. O. Box 3500
Station "A"
Sudbury, Ontario   P3A 4S2
(705) 522-7823

Temagami District
P. O. Box 38
Temagami, Ontario   P0H 2H0
(705) 569-3622

Terrace Bay District
P. O. Box 280
Terrace Bay, Ontario   P0T 2W0
(807) 825-3205

Thunder Bay District
Ontario Government Building
435 James Street South
P. O. Box 5000
Station "F"
Thunder Bay, Ontario   P7C 5G6
(807) 475-1531

Timmins District
896 Riverside Drive
Timmins, Ontario   P4N 3W2
(705) 267-7951

Tweed District
Metcalf Street
Tweed, Ontario   K0K 3J0
(613) 478-2330

Wawa District
22 Mission Road
P. O. Box 1160
Wawa, Ontario   PoS 1Ko
(705) 856-2396

Wingham District
P. O. Box 490
Highway #4 South
Wingham, Ontario   NoG 2Wo
(519) 357-3131

Appendix 3

Conservation Authority Offices

Ausable-Bayfield
P. O. Box 459
175 Thames Road West
Exeter, Ontario   NoM 1So
(519) 235-2610

Cataraqui Region
R. R. #1
Glenburnie, Ontario   KoH 1So
(613) 546-4228

Catfish Creek
R. R. #5
Aylmer, Ontario   N5H 2R4
(519) 773-9037

Central Lake Ontario
1650 Dundas Street East
Whitby, Ontario   L1N 2K8
(416) 579-0411

Credit Valley
Meadowvale, Ontario   LoJ 1Ko
(416) 451-1615

Crowe Valley
P. O. Box 416
Marmora, Ontario   KoK 2Mo
(613) 472-3137

Essex Region
360 Fairview Avenue West
Essex, Ontario   N8M 1Y6
(519) 776-5209

Ganaraska Region
P. O. Box 328
Port Hope, Ontario   L1A 3W4
(416) 885-8173

Grand River
P. O. Box 729
400 Clyde Road
Cambridge, Ontario   N1R 5W6
(519) 621-2761

Halton Region
310 Main Street
Milton, Ontario   L9T 1P4
(416) 878-4131

Hamilton Region
P. O. Box 7099
838 Mineral Springs Road
Ancaster, Ontario   L9G 3L3
(416) 525-2181

Kawartha Region
P. O. Box 819
Fenelon Falls, Ontario   K0M 1N0
(705) 887-3112

Kettle Creek
R. R. #8
St. Thomas, Ontario   N5P 3T3
(519) 631-1270

Lakehead Region
P. O. Box 3476
1136 Oliver Road
Thunder Bay, Ontario   P7B 5J9
(807) 344-5857

Long Point Region
P. O. Box 525
Simcoe, Ontario   N3Y 4N5
(519) 426-4623

Lower Thames Valley
100 Thames Street
Chatham, Ontario   N7L 2Y8
(519) 354-7310

Lower Trent Region
441 Front Street
Trenton, Ontario   K8V 6C1
(613) 394-4829

Maitland Valley
P. O. Box 5
Wroxeter, Ontario   N0G 2X0
(519) 335-3557

Mattagami Region
133 Cedar Street South
Timmins, Ontario   P4N 2G9
(705) 264-5309

Metropolitan Toronto & Region
5 Shoreham Drive
Downsview, Ontario   M3N 1S4
(416) 661-6600

Mississippi Valley
P. O. Box 268
Lanark, Ontario   K0G 1K0
(613) 259-2421

Moira River
217 North Front Street
Belleville, Ontario   K8P 3C3
(613) 968-3434

Napanee Region
25 Ontario Street West
Napanee, Ontario   K7R 3S6
(613) 354-3312

Niagara Peninsula
P. O. Box 460
Fonthill, Ontario   L0S 1E0
(416) 892-2621

Nickel District
West Tower, Civic Centre Square
200 Brady Street
Sudbury, Ontario   P3E 5K3
(705) 674-5249

North Bay − Mattawa
P. O. Box 1215
348 Fraser Street
North Bay, Ontario   P1B 8K4
(705) 474-5420

North Grey Region
P. O. Box 759
Owen Sound, Ontario   N4K 5W9
(519) 376-3076

Nottawasaga Valley
R. R. #1
Angus, Ontario   L0M 1B0
(705) 424-1479

Otonabee Region
727 Landsdowne Street West
Peterborough, Ontario   K9J 1Z2
(705) 745-5791

Prince Edward Region
P. O. Box 310
Picton, Ontario   K0K 2T0
(613) 476-7408

Raisin Region
P. O. Box 10
Martintown, Ontario   K0C 1S0
(613) 528-4584

Rideau Valley
P. O. Box 599
Mill Street
Manotick, Ontario   K0A 2N0
(613) 692-3571

Sauble Valley
P. O. Box 759
Owen Sound, Ontario   N4K 5W9
(519) 376-3076

Saugeen Valley
R. R. #1
Hanover, Ontario   N4N 3B8
(519) 364-1255

Sault Ste. Marie Region
99 Foster Drive
Civic Centre
Sault Ste. Marie, Ontario   P6A 5X6
(705) 949-9111

South Lake Simcoe
P. O. Box 282
120 Bayview Avenue
Newmarket, Ontario   L3Y 4X1
(416) 895-1281

South Nation River
P. O. Box 69
Berwick, Ontario   K0C 1G0
(613) 984-2400

St. Clair Region
205 Mill Pond Crescent
Strathroy, Ontario   N7G 3P9
(519) 245-3710

Upper Thames River
P. O. Box 6278
Station "D"
London, Ontario   N5W 5S1
(519) 451-2800

Other Reading

Acerrans, Anthony J.: *The Outdoorsman's Emergency Manual*. Stoeger
    Publishing Co., South Hackensack, N.J. 1976.
Angier, Bradford: *Field Guide to Edible Wild Plants*. Stackpole Books,
    Harrisburg, Pa. 1971.
Barker, Harriet: *Supermarket Backpacker*. Contemporary Books, Chicago,
    Ill. 1977.
Barker, Harriet: *The One Burner Gourmet*. Contemporary Books,
    Chicago, Ill. 1981.
Brown, Tom Jr. and Brandt Morgan: *Tom Brown's Field Guide to
    Wilderness Survival*. Berkley Books, New York, N.Y. 1983.
Bruce Trail Association: *A Manual for Group Hiking on the Bruce Trail*.
    The Bruce Trail Association, Hamilton, Ont. 1982.
Bruce Trail Association: *The Bruce Trail Guidebook, 14th Edition*. The
    Bruce Trail Association, Hamilton, Ont. 1983. (Revised every
    two to three years.)
Bruce Trail Association: *A Guide to Cross-Country Skiing on the Bruce Trail,
    2nd Edition*. The Bruce Trail Association, Hamilton, Ont. 1982.
Brunnelle, Hans: *Food for Knapsackers*. Sierra Club Books, San Francisco,
    Calif. 1971.
Budge, Anne: *Fit to Eat: A Collection of Recipes for Active People*. Boston
    Mills Press, Erin, Ont. 1983.
Chapman, L. J. and D. F. Putnam: *The Physiography of Southern Ontario,
    2nd Edition*. University of Toronto Press, Toronto, Ont. 1966.
Cobb, Boughton: *A Field Guide to the Ferns and their Related Families*.
    Houghton Mifflin Company, Boston, Mass. 1963.
Cornell, Joseph Bharat: *Sharing Nature with Children*. Ananda
    Publications. 1979.
Cunningham, Gerry and Margaret Hansson: *Lightweight Camping
    Equipment and How to Make It*. Charles Scribners' Sons, New York,
    N.Y. 1976.
Danielsen, John A.: *Winter Camping*. Adirondac Mountain Club,
    Glen Falls, N.Y. 1982.
Doan, Marlyn: *Starting Small in the Wilderness: The Sierra Club Outdoors
    Guide for Families*. Sierra Club Books, San Francisco, Calif. 1979.

Dorsey, June: *Games (and More) for Backpackers*. Putnam Publishing Co., New York, N.Y. 1979.

Fleming, June: *Staying Found*. Vintage Press, New York, N.Y. 1982.

Fleming, June: *The Well-Fed Backpacker*. Vintage Press, New York, N.Y. 1981.

Fry, Alan: *Survival in the Wilderness*. Macmillan of Canada, Toronto, Ont. 1981.

Forgey, William W., M.D.: *Forgey's Wilderness Medicine*. Indiana Camp Supply Books, Pittsboro, Ind. 1979.

Frisbie, Richard: *It's a Wise Woodsman Who Knows What's Biting Him: Advice for the Weekend Outdoorsman*. Doubleday & Co., Garden City, N.J. 1969.

Gale, Bill: *The Wonderful World of Walking*. William Morrow & Co., New York, N.Y. 1979.

Gibbons, Euell: *Stalking the Wild Asparagus*. David McKay Co., New York, N.Y. 1970. (How to find and cook edible wild plants).

Hart, John: *Walking Softly in the Wilderness: The Sierra Club Guide to Backpacking*. Sierra Club Books, San Francisco, Calif. 1977.

Hosie, R. C.: *Native Trees of Canada*. Queen's Printer for Canada, Ottawa, Ont. 1969.

Judd, W. W. and J. Murray Spiers: *A Naturalist's Guide to Ontario*. University of Toronto Press for the Federation of Ontario Naturalists, Toronto, Ont. 1964.

Krohn, Michael: *Photography for the Hiker and Backpacker*. Ptarmigan Press, Seattle, Wash. 1979.

Macklin, Harvey: *The Backpacker's Cookbook*. Pagurian Press, Toronto, Ont. 1978.

Maughan, Jackie Johnson and Ann Puddicombe: *Hiking the Backcountry: A Do-it-Yourself Guide for the Adventurous Woman*. Stackpole Books Inc., Harrisburg, Pa. 1981.

McQuilkin, Robert: *Comfort Below Freezing: An Introduction to the Art of Winter Camping*. Anderson World Inc., Mountain View, Calif. 1980.

Nichols, Maggie: *Wild, Wild Woman: A Complete Woman's Guide to Enjoying the Great Outdoors*. Berkley Publishing, New York, N.Y. 1978.

Niering, William A. and Nancy C. Olmstead: *The Audubon Society Field Guide to North American Wildflowers. Eastern Region*. Alfred A. Knopf, New York, N.Y. 1970.

Paul, Arleen: *Kids Camping.* Pocket Books, New York, N.Y. 1975.

Peterson, Lee Allen: *A Field Guide to Edible Wild Plants: Eastern/Central North America.* Houghton Mifflin Company, Boston, Mass. 1977.

Peterson, Roger Tory: *A Field Guide to the Birds East of the Rockies.* Houghton Mifflin Company, Boston, Mass. 1980.

Peterson, Roger Tory and Margaret McKenney: *A Field Guide to the Wildflowers of Northeastern and North-Central North America.* Houghton Mifflin Company, Boston, Mass. 1968.

Roberts, Harry: *Keeping Warm and Dry.* Stonewall Press, Boston, Mass. 1982.

Rood, Ronald: *It's Going to Sting Me! A Coward's Guide to the Great Outdoors.* McGraw Hill, Toronto, Ont. 1976.

Schifman, Ted and Susan Lariviere: *Amphoto Guide to Backpacking Photography.* American Photographic Book Publishing, New York, N.Y. 1981.

Simer, Peter and John Sullivan: *The National Outdoor Leadership School's Wilderness Guide.* Simon and Schuster, New York, N.Y. 1983.

Singleton, Capt. Robert R.: *You'll Never Get Lost Again: Simple Navigation for Everyone.* Winchester Press, New York, N.Y. 1979.

Smith, Roger: *The Penguin Book of Orienteering.* Penguin Books, Markham, Ont. 1982.

St. John Ambulance: *First Aid: Safety Oriented.* St. John Ambulance, Ottawa, Ont. 1983.

Stokes, Donald W.: *A Guide to Nature in Winter, Northeast and North-Central North America.* Little, Brown and Company, Boston, Mass. 1976.

Stout, James H. and Ann M. Stout: *Backpacking with Small Children.* Fitzhenry and Whiteside, Toronto, Ont. 1975.

Waterman, Laura and Guy Waterman: *Backwoods Ethics: Environmental Concerns for Hikers and Campers.* Stonewall Press, Boston, Mass. 1979.

Wilkinson, James A., M.D.: *Medicine for Mountaineering.* The Mountaineers, Seattle, Wash. 1975.

Wood, Robert S.: *The 2oz Backpacker: A Problem Solving Manual for Use in the Wilds.* Ten Speed Press, Berkeley, Calif. 1982.

Zakreski, L. A.: *The Budget Backpacker. How to Select or Make, Maintain and Repair Your Own Lightweight Backpacking and Camping Equipment.* Winchester Press, New York, N.Y. 1977.

The Best Hiking in Ontario

Edited by Sarah Reid
Designed by David John Shaw
Composed by Accurate Typesetting Ltd.
Manufactured by Gagné Printing Ltd.

Printed and bound in Canada
1984